W9-CNV-437

# MINUTE
## GUIDE TO
# PowerPoint

Joe Kraynak

## alpha
## books

*A Division of Prentice Hall Computer Publishing*

*201 West 103rd Street, Indianapolis, Indiana 46290 USA*

# ©1994 by Alpha Books

All rights reserved. No part of this book shall be reproduced, stored in a retrieval system, or transmitted by any means, electronic, mechanical, photocopying, recording, or otherwise, without written permission from the publisher. No patent liability is assumed with respect to the use of the information contained herein. Although every precaution has been taken in the preparation of this book, the publisher and author assume no responsibility for errors or omissions. Neither is any liability assumed for damages resulting from the use of the information contained herein. For information, address Alpha Books, 201 West 103rd Street, Indianapolis, Indiana 46290.

International Standard Book Number: 1-56761-423-X

Library of Congress Catalog Card Number: 93-73897

96 95 94   8 7 6 5 4 3

Interpretation of the printing code: the rightmost number of the second series of numbers is the number of the book's printing. For example, a printing code of 94-1 shows that the first printing of the book occurred in 1994.

*Printed in the United States of America*

All terms mentioned in this book that are known to be trademarks have been appropriately capitalized. Alpha Books cannot attest to the accuracy of this information. Use of a term in this book should not be regarded as affecting the validity of any trademark or service mark.

*Screen reproductions in this book were created by means of the program Collage Plus from Inner Media, Inc., Hollis, NH.*

Publisher: Marie Butler-Knight
Managing Editor: Elizabeth Keaffaber
Product Development Manager: Faithe Wempen
Acquisitions Manager: Barry Pruett
Development Editor: Seta Frantz
Manuscript Editor: San Dee Phillips
Book Designer: Roger Morgan
Index: Jeanne Clark
Production: Gary Adair, Katy Bodenmiller, Brad Chinn, Kim Cofer, Meshell Dinn, Mark Enochs, Stephanie Gregory, Jenny Kucera, Beth Rago, Marc Shecter, Kris Simmons, Greg Simsic, Carol Stamile

*Special Thanks to C. Herbert Feltner for ensuring the technical accuracy of this book.*

# Contents

# Introduction

You may have heard that PowerPoint is powerful and easy to use, and that it allows you to quickly create and modify slide and overhead presentations and create printouts of your presentations. But now that you have the program, where do you start?

A few things are certain:

- You need to learn the program quickly.

- You need to identify and learn only the information necessary to perform a specific task.

- You need some clear-cut, plain-English instructions that tell you what to do.

Welcome to the *10 Minute Guide to PowerPoint*.

## What Is a 10 Minute Guide?

The *10 Minute Guide* series is a new approach to learning computer programs. Like all *10 Minute Guides*, this one is divided into a series of over 20 lessons, each designed to be completed in 10 minutes or less. Each lesson is a self-contained series of steps that teaches you how to perform a specific task.

## What Is PowerPoint?

PowerPoint is a *presentation graphics program*. That is, it allows you to place text, art, and graphs on *slides* to create a slide show. The slide show can then be printed, displayed on-screen, or transformed into 35mm slides or overhead transparencies. A sample slide is shown in Figure I.1.

**Figure I.1**   A sample slide created with PowerPoint.

## Understanding Presentations

A *presentation* is a collection of slides designed to present an idea, prove a point, or convince an audience to take some action. With PowerPoint, you can create the slides you want to include in the presentation in any order. PowerPoint provides the tools you need to rearrange the slides later.

## Speaker's Notes and Audience Handouts

In addition to creating slides, you can use PowerPoint to create speaker's notes pages and audience handouts. Each speaker's notes page can include a copy of one of the slides in the presentation plus any details the speaker wants to point out.

Audience handouts contain copies of all the slides including any text that the presenter wants to add. Handouts provide the audience with a way of reviewing the material later.

## Conventions Used in This Book

Each mini-lesson in this book is set up in an easily accessible format. Steps that you must perform are numbered. Pictures of screens show you what to expect. And the following icons point out definitions, warnings, and tips to help you understand what you're doing and avoid trouble:

**Plain English** icons appear wherever a new term is defined.

**Panic Button** icons appear where new users commonly run into trouble.

**Timesaver Tips** offer shortcuts and hints for using the program effectively.

**Version 4** icons point out the new features introduced in PowerPoint 4.0.

In addition, the following conventions are used to provide a clear idea of what to do:

| | |
|---|---|
| **What you type** | The information you type appears in bold and in color. |
| Keys you press or items you select | If you are told to press a key or select an item, the key or item appears in color. If the item has an underlined selection letter, that letter appears in bold color. |
| **On-screen text** | Any text that appears on-screen is printed in bold. |
| Menu names | Whenever we mention the name of a menu or screen, the first letter of its name is capitalized. |

## How to Use This Book

If you are new to Microsoft Windows, work through the Windows primer at the back of this book. This primer leads you through the Windows basics, explaining how to use the mouse and how to enter commands in Windows.

If you haven't yet installed PowerPoint, turn to the inside front cover of this book for installation instructions.

Once you know the Windows basics and have installed PowerPoint, you can work through this book from Lesson 1 to the end, or skip to any lesson in the book, as needed.

# Lesson

# Starting and Exiting PowerPoint

*In this lesson, you will learn how to start and exit Microsoft PowerPoint.*

## Starting PowerPoint

Before you start PowerPoint, you should have a basic understanding of how to get around in Microsoft Windows. If you need a refresher course in Windows, read the Windows Primer at the back of this book. To start PowerPoint, perform the following steps:

1. Start Windows, and display the Program Manager.

2. If the Microsoft Office program group is not displayed, click on Window in the menu bar, and select Microsoft Office.

   > **No Microsoft Office Window?** The PowerPoint application icon may be in a different program group window, depending on how you installed it.

3. Double-click on the Microsoft PowerPoint icon, as shown in Figure 1.1, or use the arrow keys to highlight the icon, and press Enter. PowerPoint starts, and the Tip of the Day dialog box appears.

Double click on this icon.

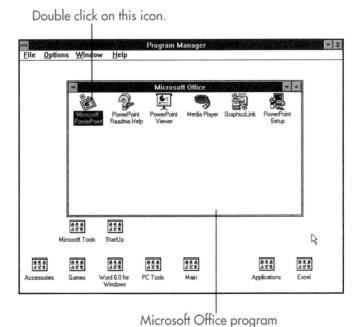

Microsoft Office program group window

**Figure 1.1** Double-click on the Microsoft PowerPoint application icon.

**4.** (Optional) To prevent the Tip of the Day from appearing when you start PowerPoint, click on the Show Tips at Startup check box. The X in the check box will disappear.

**5.** Click on the OK button. The Tip of the Day dialog box disappears, and the PowerPoint dialog box appears, prompting you to create a new presentation. (See Figure 1.2.)

> **Creating a New Presentation** The PowerPoint dialog box is designed to lead you through the process of creating a new presentation. For details on how to use this dialog box, see Lesson 2.

The Help button

PowerPoint dialog box

**Figure 1.2**   PowerPoint can lead you through the process of creating a new presentation.

## Getting Help

PowerPoint offers several help features that can teach you how to perform a simple task or use an advanced feature:

**Help menu**   Open the Help menu, and select Contents (for groups of help topics), Search for Help on (to search for a specific topic), Index (for a list of help topics from A to Z), Quick Preview (to view an on-line demonstration), Tip of the Day (to view a time-saving tip), Cue Cards (to display step-by-step instructions for a task), Technical Support (for information on what to do when all else fails), or About Microsoft PowerPoint (for licensing and system information).

**F1 Key**   Press the F1 key anytime to see the Help Table of Contents. If you press F1 when a dialog box is displayed, PowerPoint displays help that relates to that dialog box.

**Help button**   At the right end of the Standard toolbar is the Help button. It has an arrow and a question mark on it. Click on this button, and then click on the object or command about which you want more information.

**Tip of the Day**   The Tip of the Day dialog box appears each time you start PowerPoint. You can display this dialog box at any time by opening the **Help** menu and selecting Ti**p** of the Day. Click on the Next Tip button to see additional tips.

**Cue Cards**   Cue cards are like cheat sheets that appear on-screen and explain, step-by-step, how to perform a task. To display Cue Cards, open the Help menu and select Cue Cards. Click on the button for the task you want to perform.

**Quick Preview**   If you like to learn by watching a brief demonstration, open the Help menu and choose Quick Preview. A list of features appears. Select the feature you want PowerPoint to demonstrate, and then sit back and watch.

## Navigating the Help System

Most help windows contain *jumps* that let you get more information about related topics. If you select a topic that is solid-underlined, PowerPoint will open a Help window for that topic. If you select a term that is dotted-underlined, PowerPoint displays a definition for that term (see Figure 1.3). To select a topic or term, click on it, or tab to it and press Enter.

Control-menu box

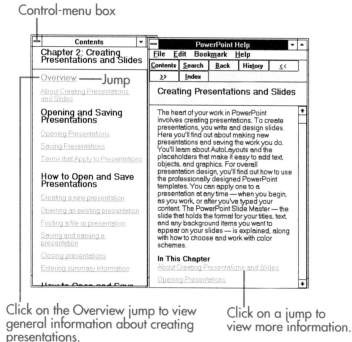

Click on the Overview jump to view
general information about creating
presentations.

Click on a jump to
view more information.

**Figure 1.3**   Jumps provide an intelligent way to move
through the Help system.

**Jumps**   A jump is a term or phrase that appears
underlined and in another color and that links one
help window to another. There are two types of
jumps: solid and dotted underlined. Solid underlined
jumps display a new help screen. Dotted underline
jumps display the definition for a term.

## Using the Help Buttons

At the top of the Help window is the following series of buttons
that allow you to move around the Help system. To use one of
the buttons, click on it, or press the key that corresponds to the
highlighted character in the button's name.

**Contents**   Displays a list of Help topics from which you can choose.

**Search**   Lets you search for a Help topic by typing the topic's name or part of its name.

**Back**   Takes you back to the previous Help window.

**History**   Displays a list of Help topics you most recently looked at.

**Index**   Displays an alphabetical listing of Help topics.

**<<**   Goes back to a previous Help screen in a related series of Help screens.

**>>**   Displays the next Help screen in a related series of Help screens.

> **Leaving the Help System**   To exit the Help system, double-click on the Control-menu box in the upper left corner of the Help window, or click anywhere inside the window and press Alt+F4. You can also exit by selecting the Exit command from the File menu.

## Exiting PowerPoint

To leave PowerPoint, perform the following steps:

**1.** If the PowerPoint dialog box is on-screen, click on the Cancel button to close it.

**2.** Do one of the following:

- Open the File menu, and select Exit.
- Press Alt+F4.

- Double-click on PowerPoint's Control-menu button (the small box at the upper left corner of the screen).

In this lesson, you learned how to start and exit PowerPoint and how to get on-line help. In the next lesson, you will learn how to create a presentation using the PowerPoint dialog box.

# Lesson

# Creating a New Presentation

*In this lesson, you will learn how to create a presentation in four different ways.*

## Starting a New Presentation

If you just started PowerPoint, and the PowerPoint dialog box is displayed, you are ready to start a new presentation. If the PowerPoint dialog box is not displayed, perform the following steps:

1. Click on File in the menu bar.

2. Click on New. The New Presentation dialog box appears as shown in Figure 2.1.

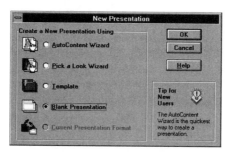

**Figure 2.1** The New Presentation dialog box provides five simple ways to create a new presentation.

**Quick New File**   To bypass the File menu, click on the New button in the Standard toolbar. The New button is the leftmost button just under the menu bar.

The PowerPoint dialog box gives you the following five ways to create a new presentation:

**AutoContent Wizard**   Creates outlines for any of six presentations, including strategy, sales, and training presentations. The presentation acts as a rough draft, which you can edit and enhance.

**Pick a Look Wizard**   Creates a collection of slides which all have a consistent, professional look. You can add the content for the presentation later.

**Template**   Lets you build a slide show from a predesigned slide. You provide the content, and PowerPoint takes care of the appearance.

**Blank Presentation**   Allows you to start from scratch. You build the presentation by supplying both the content and design.

**Current Presentation Format**   Is available if you have a previously created presentation displayed. This option lets you create a new presentation that is based on the design of the existing presentation.

**Wizards**   Wizards are a unique feature in most Microsoft products. A wizard displays a series of dialog boxes that ask you design and content questions. You select options and type text. When you are done, the Wizard creates something (in this case, a presentation) according to your instructions.

# Using the AutoContent Wizard

With the AutoContent Wizard, you select the type of presentation you want to create (strategy, sales, training, reporting, conveying bad news, or general), and PowerPoint creates an outline for the presentation. Here's how you use the Auto-Content Wizard:

1. In the PowerPoint dialog box, click on the AutoContent Wizard option button, and then click on the OK button. The AutoContent Wizard Step 1 of 4 dialog box appears.

2. Read the dialog box, and then click on the Next button, or press Enter. The AutoContent Wizard Step 2 of 4 dialog box appears.

**Going Back**   Each Wizard dialog box contains a **B**ack button that lets you trace back through previous dialog boxes to change your selections or edit your text. Simply click on the button, or press Alt+B.

3. Type a title for the presentation. (For example, Marketing Strategy.)

4. Press Tab, and type your name or the name of the person who is going to give the presentation.

5. Press Tab, and type any other information that you want to appear on the first slide in the presentation.

6. Click on the Next button, or press Alt+N. The AutoContent Wizard Step 3 of 4 dialog box appears. (See Figure 2.2.)

7. Select the type of presentation you want to create, and then click on the Next button, or press Alt+N. The AutoContent Wizard Step 4 of 4 dialog box appears.

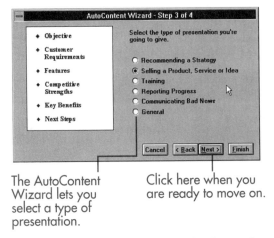

The AutoContent
Wizard lets you
select a type of
presentation.

Click here when you
are ready to move on.

**Figure 2.2** The AutoContent Wizard leads you through the process.

**8.** Click on the Finish button, or press Alt+F. The Wizard creates the presentation and displays the presentation in outline view.

**Outline View** PowerPoint can display a presentation in any of four views: Outline, Slide, Note, and Slide Sorter. To learn more about the different views and how to change views, see Lesson 4.

## Using the Pick a Look Wizard

The Pick a Look Wizard lets you create black-and-white or color overheads, an on-screen presentation, or 35mm slides that have a consistent and professional look. Here's what you do to run the Pick a Look Wizard:

**1.** In the PowerPoint dialog box, click on the Pick a Look Wizard option button, and then click on the OK button. The Pick a Look Wizard Step 1 of 9 dialog box appears.

**2.** Read the dialog box, and then click on the Next button, or press Alt+N. The Pick a Look Wizard Step 2 of 9 dialog box appears, providing a list of output options.

**3.** Select the desired output for your presentation, and click on the Next button. The Step 3 of 9 dialog box appears, asking you to select an overall design.

**Can't Decide on an Output?** If you cannot decide on an output, don't worry; you can select a different output option at any time.

**Limited Choice?** If you do not like any of the designs listed, click on the More button. This opens a dialog box that lets you select from a list of templates. Click on a name in the File **N**ame list, and then click on **A**pply to use the template.

**4.** Click on a design for your presentation, and then click on the Next button. The Step 4 of 9 dialog box appears.

**5.** By default, PowerPoint will create all the presentation items (slides, speaker's notes, audience handouts, and an outline). Select any items you want to exclude, and then click on the Next button. The Slide Options dialog box appears.

**6.** If you want PowerPoint to print the date, slide number, or other text on each slide, select any information you want included, and click on the Next button.

**7.** If you chose to include speaker's notes, audience handouts, and outline pages, repeat step 6 for each item in the presentation. The Step 9 of 9 dialog box appears.

**8.** Click on the Finish button. PowerPoint creates one slide that matches your design choices and displays it on-screen. (In Lesson 8, you will learn how to add slides to your presentation.)

## Using a Template

The Template option lets you select a predesigned look for your presentation. PowerPoint creates the first slide. Here's how you use a template:

**1.** In the PowerPoint or New Presentation dialog box, click on Template, and then click on the OK button. The Presentation Template dialog box appears, as shown in Figure 2.3.

Double-click on the template directory to view other subdirectories that contain templates.

Click on the Apply button when you are done.

Templates —

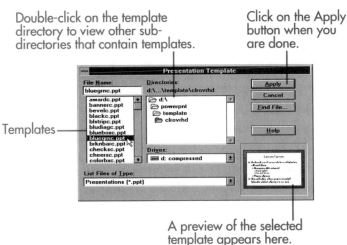

A preview of the selected template appears here.

**Figure 2.3**  Select a template from the list.

2. In the File Name list, click on a template name to see what the template looks like. The preview area shows a thumbnail view of the template.

> **More Templates**    PowerPoint has three groups of templates: black-and-white overheads, color overheads, and slides. To see a list of templates in a particular group, double-click on template in the **D**irectories list, and then double-click on the desired subdirectory (bwovrhd, clrovrhd, or sldshow).

3. When you have selected a template you like, click on the Apply button. The New Slide dialog box appears, as shown in Figure 2.4.

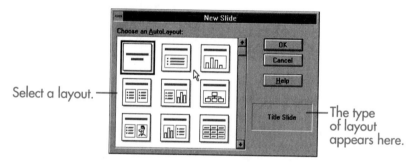

Select a layout. ──

The type of layout appears here.

**Figure 2.4**    The New Slide dialog box lets you select a structure for your slides.

4. Click on the desired layout for your slides, or use the arrow keys to select a layout.

5. Click on the OK button. PowerPoint creates a slide that has the look and structure you specified.

## Starting a Blank Presentation

If you are experienced in creating presentations, you may want to start a presentation from scratch and develop your own design and content. If so, take the following steps to create a blank presentation:

1. In the PowerPoint dialog box, click on Blank Presentation, and then click on the OK button. The New Slide dialog box appears, as shown in Figure 2.4.

2. Click on the desired layout for your slides, or use the arrow keys to select a layout.

3. Click on the OK button. PowerPoint creates a slide that has the structure you specified.

Now that you have a presentation, you can edit its text, add pictures and graphs, change the presentation's overall look, and enhance it in many other ways. The procedures you need to follow are covered in later lessons. The next lesson provides a brief tour of the PowerPoint screen and explains how to enter commands.

# Lesson

# Getting Around in PowerPoint

*In this lesson, you will learn how to get around in PowerPoint and enter commands.*

## A Look at PowerPoint's Application Window

If you created a new presentation using the AutoContent Wizard, your screen looks something like the screen shown in Figure 3.1. This screen contains many of the same elements you will find in any Windows programs: a Control-menu box, a title bar, Minimize and Restore buttons, a menu bar, and a status bar. For an explanation of these elements, refer to the Windows Primer at the back of this book.

In addition, you will see three toolbars and a presentation window that are unique to PowerPoint. The following sections explain how to work with these unique items.

**Toolbar** A toolbar is a collection of buttons that allow you to bypass the menu system. For example, instead of opening the **F**ile menu and selecting **N**ew, you can click on the New button to create a new presentation.

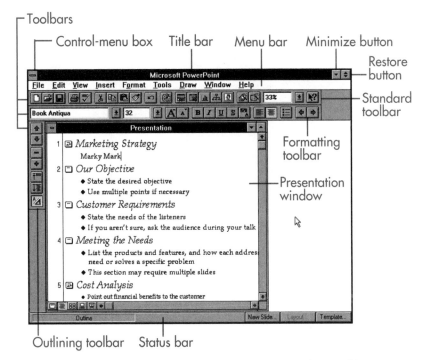

**Figure 3.1**    PowerPoint provides many tools for quickly entering commands.

## The Presentation Window

In the center of the PowerPoint window is a *presentation window.* You will use this window to create your slides and arrange the slides in a presentation. At the bottom of the presentation window are several buttons that allow you to change views. For example, Figure 3.1 shows a presentation in Outline view, whereas Figure 3.2 shows the same presentation in Slide view. For details about changing views, see Lesson 4.

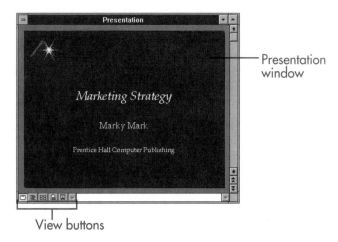

Figure 3.2  You can change views simply by clicking on a button.

## Using Shortcut Menus

Although you can enter all commands in PowerPoint by pulling down a menu and selecting the command, PowerPoint 4 offers a quicker way with context-sensitive shortcut menus. To use a shortcut menu, move the mouse pointer over the object you want the command to act on, and then click on the right mouse button. A shortcut menu pops up, as shown in Figure 3.3, offering the commands that pertain to the selected object. Click on the desired command.

## Working with Toolbars

PowerPoint displays three toolbars: the Standard and Formatting toolbars below the menu bar (see Figure 3.1), and the Outline or Drawing toolbar to the left of the presentation

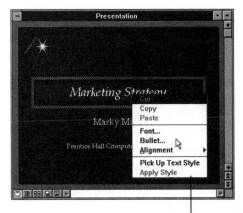

Right-click on an object to display a
context-sensitive shortcut menu.

**Figure 3.3**    Display a shortcut menu by right-clicking on an
object.

window. (The toolbar on the left varies, depending on which
view is displayed.) To select a button from the toolbar, click
on the button.

## Learning More About Toolbar Buttons

Although I could list and explain all the tools in the Standard
toolbar and in all the other toolbars, here are some better
ways to learn about the buttons for yourself:

- To see the name of a button, move the mouse
  pointer over the button. PowerPoint displays a
  *ToolTip* that provides the name of the button.

- To learn what a button does, move the mouse
  pointer over the button, and look at the status bar
  (bottom of the screen). If the button is available for
  the task you are currently performing, PowerPoint
  displays a description of what the button does.

- To learn more about a button, click on the Help button in the Standard toolbar (the button with the arrow and question mark), and then click on the button for which you want more information.

## Turning Toolbars On or Off

If you never use a particular toolbar, you can turn it off to free up some screen space. In addition, you can turn on other toolbars. To turn a toolbar on or off:

1. Open the View menu, and choose Toolbars. The Toolbars dialog box appears.

2. Select the toolbar(s) you would like to hide or display. An **X** in the toolbar's check box means the bar will be displayed.

3. Click on the OK button.

> **Use the Shortcut Menu**   A quick way to display or hide a toolbar is to use the toolbar shortcut menu. Right-click on any toolbar, and then click on the name of the toolbar you want to hide or display.

## Moving Toolbars

After you have displayed the toolbars you need, you may position them in your work area where they are most convenient. Here's what you do to move a toolbar:

1. Move the mouse pointer over a buttonless part of the toolbar.

2. Hold down the left mouse button, and Drag the toolbar where you want it:

- Drag the toolbar to a toolbar dock. There are four toolbar docks: just below the menu bar, on the left and right sides of the PowerPoint application window, and just above the status bar. If a toolbar contains a drop-down list, you cannot drag it to the left or right toolbar dock.

- Drag the toolbar anywhere inside the application window to create a *floating toolbar*.

**3.** Release the mouse button.

**Floating Toolbar**   A floating toolbar acts just like a window. You can drag its title bar to move it or drag a border to size it. If you drag a floating toolbar to a toolbar dock, the toolbar turns back into a normal (nonfloating) toolbar.

**Customizing Toolbars**   To customize a toolbar, right-click on it, and choose Customize. You can then drag a toolbar button from one toolbar to another or drag a button off a toolbar (to remove it). To add a button from the Customize Toolbars dialog box, select a feature category from the **Categories** list, and then drag the desired button to any of the toolbars.

In this lesson, you learned about the PowerPoint application and presentation windows, and you learned how to enter commands with shortcut menus and toolbars. In the next lesson, you will learn how to edit the presentation you created in Lesson 2.

# Lesson

# Working with Slides in Different Views

*In this lesson, you will learn how to display a presentation in different views, and edit slides in Outline and Slide view.*

## Changing Views

PowerPoint can display your presentation in different views that make it easier to perform certain tasks. For example, Outline view makes it easier to see the overall organization of the presentation, whereas Slide Sorter view lets you quickly rearrange the slides. Figure 4.1 shows the available views.

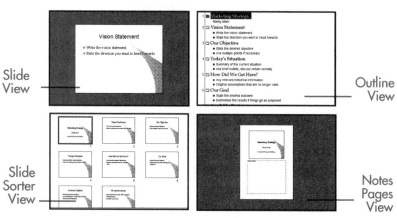

**Figure 4.1** You can change views to make a task easier.

To change views, open the View menu and choose the desired view: Slides, Outline, Slide Sorter, or Notes Pages. A quicker way to change views is to click on the button for the desired view at the bottom of the presentation window.

**Outline to Slide View**   In Outline view, you can quickly display a slide in Slide view by double-clicking on the desired slide icon in the outline.

**What About the Slide Show Option?**   The Slide Show option lets you view your presentation as a timed slide show. For details, see Lesson 21.

# Moving from Slide to Slide

When you have more than one slide in your presentation, you will need to move from one slide to the next in order to work with a specific slide. The procedure for moving to a slide depends on which view you are currently using:

* In **Outline view**, use the scroll bar to display the slide you want to work with. Click on the Slide icon (the icon to the left of the slide's title) to select the slide, or click anywhere inside the text to edit it.

* In **Slide view**, click on the Previous Slide or Next Slide button just below the vertical scroll bar, as shown in Figure 4.2, or drag the box inside the scroll bar until the desired slide number is displayed, and then release the mouse button.

* In **Slide Sorter view**, click on the desired slide. A thick border appears around the selected slide.

* In **Notes Pages view**, click on the Previous Slide or Next Slide button, or drag the box inside the scroll bar until the desired slide number is displayed, and then release the mouse button.

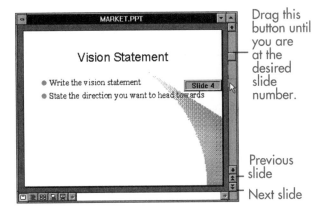

**Figure 4.2**   Use the Previous Slide and Next Slide buttons.

# Editing Slides

If you created a presentation in Lesson 2 using the AutoContent Wizard, you already have several slides, but they may not contain the text you want to use. If you used the Pick a Look Wizard or a template, or you created a blank presentation, you have one slide on-screen that you can edit.

In the following sections, you will learn the basics of how to edit text in Outline view and Slide view. In later lessons, you will learn how to add and edit text objects, pictures, graphs, organizational charts, and other items.

> **Objects**   An object is any item on a slide, including lines and boxes for text, graphics, and charts.

## Editing in Outline View

Outline view provides the easiest way to edit text. You simply click to move the insertion point where you want it, as shown in Figure 4.3, and then type your text. Use the Del key to delete characters to the right of the insertion point, or the Backspace key to delete characters to the left.

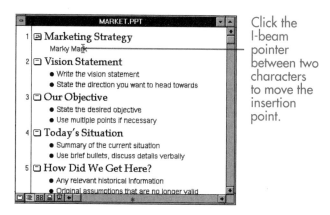

Click the I-beam pointer between two characters to move the insertion point.

**Figure 4.3**  Switch to Outline view to edit text.

To select text, hold down the left mouse button, and drag the mouse pointer over the desired text. You can then press the Del or Backspace key to delete the text, or drag the text where you want it.

> **Auto Word Select**  When you select text, PowerPoint selects whole words. If you want to select individual characters, open the Tools menu, select Options, and select Automatic Word Selection to turn it off. Click on the OK button.

## Editing in Slide View

Slide view provides an easy way to edit all objects on a slide, including text and graphic objects. As shown in Figure 4.4, you can edit an object by clicking or double-clicking on it. For a text object, click on the object to select it, and then click where you want the insertion point moved.

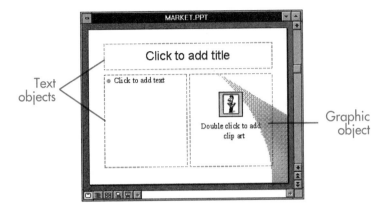

**Figure 4.4**  Slide view allows you to edit both text and graphic objects.

## Working with a Bulleted List

The bulleted list is a powerful tool for helping you to organize and present ideas and supporting data for your presentation. As you type entries, keep in mind that you can change an entry's level and position in the list. To change the position or level of an entry (in Outline view), use the arrow keys or mouse to move the insertion point anywhere inside the entry, and then perform one of the following actions:

 Click on this button to move the entry up in the list.

 Click on this button to move the entry down in the list.

 Click on this button to indent the entry to the next lower level in the list. The item will be indented, the bullet will change, and the text will usually appear smaller.

Click on this button to remove the indent and move the entry to the next higher level in the list. The item will be moved to the left, the bullet will change, and the text will appear larger.

**Dragging Paragraphs**   You can quickly change the position or level of a paragraph by dragging it up, down, left, or right. To drag a paragraph, move the mouse pointer to the left side of the paragraph until it turns into a four-headed arrow. Then, hold down the mouse button and drag the paragraph to the desired position.

In Lesson 10, you will learn how to change the appearance of the bullet, the style and size of text for each entry, and the amount the text is indented for each level.

In this lesson, you learned how to change views for a presentation, move from slide to slide, and edit text. In the next lesson, you will learn how to save, close, and open a presentation.

# Lesson

## Saving, Closing, and Opening Presentations

*In this lesson, you will learn how to save a presentation to disk, close a presentation, and open an existing presentation.*

### Saving a Presentation

Soon after creating a presentation, you should save it in a file on disk to protect the work you have already done. To save a presentation for the first time, perform the following steps:

**1.** Open the File menu, and select Save, or press Ctrl+S. The Save As dialog box appears, as shown in Figure 5.1.

> **The No-Menu Save** To bypass the File menu, click on the Save button (the button with the disk icon on it) in the Standard toolbar.

**2.** In the File Name text box, type the name you want to assign to the presentation (up to eight characters). (Do not type a file name extension; PowerPoint will automatically add the extension **.PPT**.)

**3.** To save the file to a different disk drive, pull down the Drives drop-down list, and select the letter of the drive.

Save button   Type a file name here.

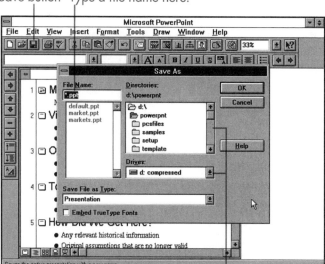

Select a drive and directory.

**Figure 5.1**   The Save As dialog box.

4. To save the file in a different directory, select the directory from the **D**irectories list.

5. Click on the **OK** button. The Summary Info dialog box appears.

6. (Optional) Type a presentation title, subject description, author name, keywords, and comments for the presentation. (This information might help you find the presentation later.)

7. Click on the OK button. The file is saved to disk.

> **Quick Resaves**   Now that you have named the file and saved it to disk, you can save any changes you make to the presentation simply by pressing Ctrl+S or clicking on the Save button in the Standard toolbar. Your data will be saved under the file name you assigned.

To create a copy of a presentation under a different name, open the File menu and select the Save As command. Use the Save As dialog box to enter a different name for the copy. You can then modify the copy without affecting the original.

## Closing a Presentation

You can close a presentation at any time. This closes the Presentation window (it does not exit PowerPoint), and allows you to use the space on-screen for a different presentation. To close a presentation, perform the following steps:

1. If more than one Presentation window is displayed, click on any portion of the window you want to close. This activates the window.

2. Open the File menu, and select Close, or press Ctrl+F4. If you have not saved the presentation, or if you haven't saved your most recent changes, a dialog box appears, asking if you want to save your changes.

3. To save your changes, click on the Yes button. If this is a new presentation, the Save As dialog box appears, as in Figure 5.1. If you have saved the file previously, your changes are saved in the file, and the Presentation window closes.

4. If the Save As dialog box appears, enter a name for the file and any other information as explained earlier. Then, click on the OK button.

## Opening a Presentation

Once you have saved a presentation to disk, you can open the presentation and continue working on it at any time. To open an existing presentation, perform the following steps:

**1.** Open the File menu, and select Open, or press Ctrl+O. The Open dialog box appears.

> **Quick Open**  To quickly open a file, click on the Open button (the button with the manila folder on it) in the Standard toolbar.

**2.** Pull down the Drives drop-down list, and select the letter of the drive on which the file is stored.

**3.** In the Directories list, select the directory in which the presentation file is stored. The list below the File Name text box displays the names of all the presentation files (files that end in .PPT) in the selected directory.

**4.** In the list below the File Name text box, click on the file you think you want to open. The first slide in the presentation appears in the preview area (see Figure 5.2).

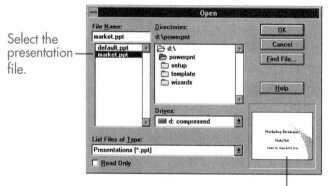

Select the presentation file.

Preview area shows the first slide in the selected presentation.

**Figure 5.2**  The Open dialog box lets you select and preview the presentation.

**5.** Double-click on the file name of the presentation you want to open, or highlight the file name and click on the OK button. PowerPoint opens the presentation.

> **Recently Opened Files**  PowerPoint keeps a list of the four most recently opened files at the bottom of the File menu. To open a file, simply select it from the File menu. You can increase the number of files listed. Open the Tools menu, and select Options. Select Entries, and type the number of files (up to 9) that you want listed.

## Finding a Presentation File

If you forgot where you saved a file, PowerPoint can help you with its new Find File feature. To have PowerPoint hunt for a file, perform the following steps:

**1.** Open the File menu, and select Find File, or click on the Find File button in the Open dialog box. You'll get the Search dialog box, as shown in Figure 5.3.

Type the name of the file you are looking for.

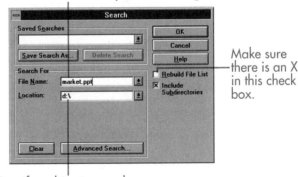

Make sure there is an X in this check box.

Specify a drive to search.

**Figure 5.3**  The Search dialog box asks you to specify what you want to search for.

**Find File Dialog Box?**    If you get the Find
File dialog box (instead of the Search dialog
box), click on the Search button at the bottom of
the Find File dialog box.

**2.** In the File **N**ame text box, type the name of the file
you are looking for. You can use wild-card characters in place of characters you can't remember. Use
an asterisk * in place of a group of characters, or use
a question mark ? in place of a single character. For
example, **\*.ppt** finds all files with the extension
.PPT, and **sales??.ppt** finds all files such as
SALES01.PPT, SALES02.PPT, and so on.

**3.** In the Location text box, type the drive and directory you want to search. For example, if you type
**c:\**, PowerPoint will search the entire C drive. Type
**c:\powerpnt**, and PowerPoint searches only the
POWERPNT directory on drive C.

**4.** To have PowerPoint search all subdirectories of the
directory you specify, select Include Subdirectories
to place an **X** in the check box.

**5.** Click on the **R**ebuild File List option to place an **X**
in its check box. This ensures that PowerPoint will
perform a fresh search.

**6.** Don't worry about the Clear option. It clears out
anything you may have typed in the File **N**ame and
**L**ocation text boxes.

**7.** Click on the **OK** button. PowerPoint finds the files
that match the search instructions you entered and
displays them in the Find File dialog box as shown
in Figure 5.4.

**8.** Look through the list, highlight the file you want,
and click on the Open button.

A list of the files that were found.

When you highlight a file name, PowerPoint displays the first file in the presentation.

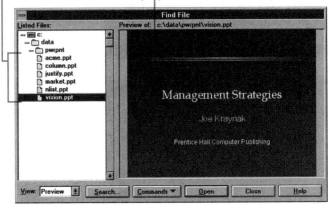

**Figure 5.4** The Find File dialog box shows a list of found files.

In this lesson, you learned how to save, close, and open presentations. In the next lesson, you will learn how to print a presentation.

# Lesson

# Printing Your Presentation

*In this lesson, you will learn how to select a size and orientation for the slides in your presentation and how to print the slides, notes, and handouts you created.*

**Notes and Handouts** The instructions in this lesson tell you how to print slides, notes, and handouts. To create audience handouts and speaker's notes pages, see Lesson 22 and 23.

## Setting Up for Printing

Before you print your presentation, you should check the slide setup to determine if the selected output, size, and orientation are suitable for your needs. Perform the following steps:

1. Open the File menu, and select Slide Setup. The Slide Setup dialog box appears, as shown in Figure 6.1.

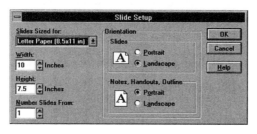

**Figure 6.1** The Slide Setup dialog box lets you set the position and size of the slides.

**2.** Click on the arrow to the right of the **S**lides Sized
for list, and select the desired output for your slides.
(For example, you can have the slides sized for 8.5-
by-11-inch paper, 35mm slides, or an on-screen slide
show.)

**3.** (Optional) To create a custom size, enter the desired dimensions in the **W**idth and **H**eight text
boxes. If you change a setting in either of these
boxes, Custom is automatically selected in the
Slides Sized for list.

> **Spin Boxes** To the right of the **W**idth and
> **H**eight text boxes are arrows that allow you to
> adjust the settings in those boxes. Click on the up
> arrow to increase the setting by .1-inch, or click on
> the down arrow to decrease the setting by .1-inch.

**4.** In the **N**umber Slides From text box, type the
number at which you want to start slide numbering.
(This is usually 1, but may differ if this presentation
is a continuation of another presentation.)

**5.** In the Orientation group, select an option to specify
how you want the slides, notes, and handouts
positioned on the page.

> **Orientation** The Orientation settings tell
> PowerPoint whether to print the slides sideways
> (in landscape orientation) or in normal (portrait)
> orientation.

**6.** Click on the OK button. If you changed the orientation setting, you may have to wait while PowerPoint
repositions the slides.

## Selecting a Printer

If you have only one printer, and you already use it for all
your Windows applications, you do not have to select a
printer (just use the printer you set up in Windows). However, if you use two printers, you should specify which
printer you want to use (for example, you may want to use a
color printer for overhead transparencies and a black-and-
white printer for speaker's notes).

To select a printer, perform the following steps:

**1.** Open the File menu, and select Print. The Print
dialog box appears. The name of the currently
selected printer appears at the top of the dialog
box.

**2.** To use a different printer, click on the Printer
button. The Print Setup dialog box appears, as
shown in Figure 6.2.

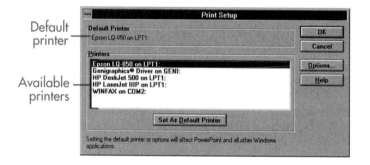

**Figure 6.2** The Print Setup dialog box shows a list of
installed printers.

**3.** In the Printers list, click on the name of the printer you want to use, or use the arrow keys to highlight it.

> **Genigraphics**    The Genigraphics option in the **P**rinters list allows you to print your presentation to a file that you can later send (on disk or via modem) to the Genigraphics service. This service converts your presentation into slides or overhead transparencies.

**4.** (Optional) To make the printer you selected the default printer for all Windows applications, click on the Set As Default Printer button.

**5.** Click on the OK button. PowerPoint returns you to the Print dialog box and shows the name of the currently selected printer.

> **Options**    The **O**ptions button in the Print Setup dialog box opens a dialog box that gives you more control over your printer. For example, you can set the print quality, select a font cartridge (if your printer uses font cartridges), and select a paper source. If you are using the Genigraphics service, the options allow you to specify the type of film or transparencies you want made.

## Printing Your Presentation

Once you have set up your slides and selected a printer, you can print your presentation. Perform the following steps:

**1.** Make sure the presentation file you want to print is displayed on-screen.

**2.** If the Print dialog box is not displayed, open the
File menu, and select Print. Figure 6.3 shows the
Print dialog box.

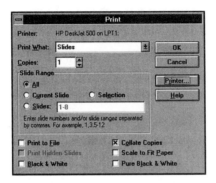

**Figure 6.3**  The Print dialog box

**3.** Click on the arrow to the right of the Print What
text box, and select the item you want to print (for
example, your slides, handouts, or speaker notes).

**4.** In the Copies text box, type the number of copies
you want printed.

**5.** In the Slide Range group, select one of the following options to specify which slides you want to
print:

**All** prints every slide in the presentation.

**Current Slide** prints only the slide that is selected or
displayed.

**Slides** prints one or more slides as instructed. To
print a single slide, type its number. To print a
range, type the first page number, a dash, and then
the last page number (for example, 4–8). To print
more than one range, separate the ranges with
commas (for example, 2,4–8,10).

**6.** (Optional) Select any of the following options at the bottom of the Print dialog box:

Print to **F**ile prints the presentation to a file on disk so you can print it later or print it using a different computer that does not have PowerPoint installed.

Print **H**idden Slides prints slides that you may have marked as hidden. For more details about hidden slides, see Lesson 20.

**B**lack & White prints color slides in black and white. This is useful for printing drafts of slides.

C**o**llate Copies is useful if you are printing two or more copies of your slides. With this option on, PowerPoint prints one full copy of the presentation before printing the next copy. With this option off, PowerPoint prints all copies of slide 1, then all copies of slide 2, and so on.

Scale to Fit **P**aper instructs PowerPoint to resize the slides automatically to fit the paper size you selected in the Slide Setup dialog box.

Pure Bl**a**ck & White prints the text and lines in black and white, without color or shading.

**7.** Click on the OK button. PowerPoint prints the specified slides.

In this lesson, you learned how to specify the dimensions and orientation of your slides, and how to print slides, audience handouts, and speaker notes. In the next lesson, you will learn how to change the overall appearance of the slides in a presentation.

# Lesson

# Changing a Presentation's Look

*In this lesson, you will learn various ways to give your presentation a professional and consistent look.*

## Giving Your Slides a Professional Look

PowerPoint comes with 150 professionally designed slides you can use as *templates* for your own presentations. That is, you can apply one of these predesigned slides to your own presentation, to give the slides in your presentation the same look as the professional slides.

**What Is a Template?** A template is a predesigned slide that comes with PowerPoint. It contains a color scheme and a general layout for each slide in the presentation. The template makes it easy for you to create a presentation; you simply fill in the blanks on each slide.

Each template has a *Slide Master* that works in the background to control the background color, layout, and style of each slide in the presentation. This provides all the slides in your presentation with a consistent look. In the following sections, you will learn various ways to apply templates and modify the look of your presentation.

# Using the Pick a Look Wizard

The Pick a Look Wizard leads you through the process of selecting a template, customizing slides, and adding headers and footers to slides, speaker's notes, audience handouts, and outlines. You can use the Pick a Look Wizard to create a new presentation, as explained in Lesson 2, or to modify an existing presentation. To modify a presentation, do the following:

1. Open the Format menu, and select Pick a Look Wizard, or click on the Pick a Look Wizard button in the Standard toolbar. The Pick a Look Wizard Step 1 of 9 dialog box appears.

2. Enter any preferences you have, and then click on the Next button.

3. Repeat step 2 for each dialog box that appears. (Refer to Lesson 2 for details.)

4. When the Step 9 of 9 dialog box appears, click on the Finish button.

> **More Color and Shading Control**   Each template has preset color and background settings. For details on how to modify the color or background of your presentation, refer to Lesson 19.

# Using a Presentation Template

You do not have to run the Pick a Look Wizard to apply a template to a presentation. You can simply select a template by doing the following:

1. Open the Format menu, and select Presentation Template. The Presentation Template dialog box appears.

**The Template Button**   To bypass the Format menu, click on the Template button on the right end of the status bar.

**2.** In the Directories list, change to the \POWERPNT\TEMPLATE directory. The template subdirectories appear. Each subdirectory contains a set of templates for a particular type of presentation: black-and-white overheads, color overheads, and slide shows.

**3.** Double-click on the template subdirectory for the type of presentation you want to create. A list of templates appears in the File Name list.

**4.** Click on a file name in the list, or tab to the list and use the ↓ key to highlight a name. When you highlight the name of a template, a slide appears in the preview area, showing what the template looks like. (See Figure 7.1.)

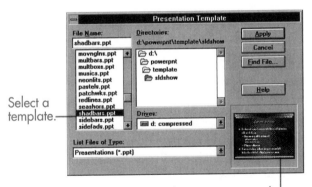

Select a template.

The preview area shows the selected template.

**Figure 7.1**   The Presentation Template dialog box lets you preview a template before you apply it.

**5.** When the desired template is highlighted, press Enter, or click on the Apply button. You are returned to your presentation, and the template is now in control of your presentation.

**Apply Templates at Any Time** You do not have to apply a template before you begin creating your presentation. You can change the template at any time, and your entire presentation will take on the look of the new template.

## Using AutoLayouts

While templates allow you to change the color and design of a presentation, AutoLayouts allow you to set the structure of a single slide in a presentation. For example, if you want a graph and a picture on a slide, you can choose an AutoLayout that positions the two items for you. To use an AutoLayout, do the following:

**1.** In Slide view, display the slide whose layout you want to change.

**2.** Open the Format menu, and select Slide Layout. The Slide Layout dialog box appears.

**Right-Click** A quick way to display the Slide Layout dialog box is to right-click on the slide in Slide view, and then select Slide Layout.

**3.** Click on the desired layout, or use the arrow keys to move the selection border to it.

**4.** Click on the Apply button. PowerPoint applies the selected layout to the current slide.

# Editing the Slide Master

Every presentation has a Slide Master that controls the overall appearance and layout of each slide. A sample Slide Master is shown in Figure 7.2.

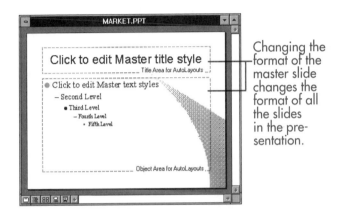

**Figure 7.2**   The Slide Master ensures that all slides in a presentation have a consistent look.

The two most important elements on the Slide Master are the *Title Area* and *Object Area* for the AutoLayout objects. The Title Area contains the formatting specifications for each slide's title; that is, it tells PowerPoint the type size, style, and color to use for the text in the title of each slide. The Object Area contains the formatting specifications for all remaining text on the slide. For most of PowerPoint's templates, the Object Area sets up specifications for a bulleted list: these include the type of bullet, as well as the type styles, sizes, and indents for each item in the list.

In addition to the Title and Object Areas, the Slide Master can contain the background color, a border, a code that inserts page numbers, your company logo, a clip art object, and any other elements you want to appear on *every* slide in the presentation.

To view the Slide Master for a presentation, perform the following steps:

1. Open the View menu, and select Master. The Master submenu appears.

2. Select Slide Master. The Slide Master appears, as shown in Figure 7.2.

3. To return to slide view, open the View menu and select Slides, or click on the Slide View button at the bottom of the presentation window.

The Slide Master is like any slide. In the following lessons, when you learn how to add text, graphics, borders, and other objects to a slide, keep in mind that you can add these objects on individual slides or on the Slide Master. When you add the objects to the Slide Master, the objects will appear on *every* slide in the presentation.

In this lesson, you learned how to give your presentation a consistent look by applying a template to it and by using the Pick a Look Wizard. You also learned how to display the Slide Master. In the next lesson, you will learn how to insert, delete, and copy slides.

# Lesson

# Inserting, Deleting, and Copying Slides

*In this lesson, you will learn how to insert new slides, delete slides, and copy slides in a presentation.*

## Inserting a Slide

You can insert a slide into a presentation at any time and at any position in the presentation. Perform the following steps:

1. Select the slide after which you want the new slide inserted. (You can select the slide in any view: Outline, Slides, Slide Sorter, or Notes Pages.)

2. Open the Insert menu, and select New Slide, or press Ctrl+M. In Outline view, PowerPoint inserts a blank slide, allowing you to type a title and bulleted list. In all other views, the New Slide dialog box appears.

> **New Slide Button**   To quickly insert a new slide, click on the New Slide button on the right end of the status bar or the Insert New Slide button in the Standard toolbar.

3. In the Choose an AutoLayout list, click on the desired slide layout, or use the arrow keys to highlight it.

**4.** Click on the OK button. PowerPoint inserts a slide that has the specified layout. See Figure 8.1.

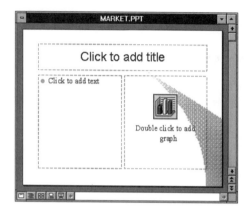

**Figure 8.1** The new slide contains the structure; you must supply the content.

**5.** Follow the directions on the slide to add text or other objects. In most cases, you must click on an object to select it and then type your entry.

**Cloning a Slide** To create an exact replica of a slide, select the slide you want to duplicate. Open the **E**dit menu, and select **D**uplicate, or press Ctrl+D. The new slide is inserted after the original slide.

## Adding Slides from Another Presentation

If you want to add all the slides from another presentation to the current presentation, perform the following steps:

**1.** Open the presentation in which you want the slides added.

**2.** Select the slide after which you want the slides added.

**3.** Open the Insert menu, and select Slides from File. The Insert File dialog box appears.

**4.** Pull down the Drives drop-down list, and select the letter of the drive on which the presentation file is stored.

**5.** In the **Directories** list, select the directory in which the presentation file is stored.

**6.** In the list below the File **Name** text box, click on the file you think you want to open. The first slide in the presentation appears in the preview area.

**7.** Double-click on the file name of the presentation whose slides you want to insert, or highlight the file name and click on the OK button. PowerPoint inserts the slides after the currently selected slide. The new slides take on the look of the current presentation.

**Taking an Outline from a Document**   If you created a document using a word-processing program and included headings in it, PowerPoint can pull the headings from the document and use them to create slides with bulleted lists. To create slides from a document, open the Insert menu, and choose Slides from Outline. Use the Insert Outline dialog box to select the document file you want to use, and then click on the OK button.

## Selecting Slides

In the following sections, you will be deleting, copying, and moving slides. However, before you can move one or more slides, you have to select the slide(s), as follows:

- To select a single slide, click on it. (In Slide or Notes Pages view, the currently displayed slide is selected; you don't have to click on it.)

- To select two or more neighboring slides (in Outline view only), click on the first slide, and then hold down the Ctrl and Shift keys while clicking on the last slide in the group.

- To select two or more non-neighboring slides (in Slide Sorter or Outline view), hold down the Shift key while clicking on each slide.

## Deleting Slides

You can delete a slide from any view. Perform the following steps:

**1.** Display the slide you want to delete (in Slide or Notes Pages view), or select the slide(s) (in Outline or Slide Sorter view).

**2.** Open the Edit menu, and select Delete Slide. The selected slide(s) is removed.

> **Oops!**   If you deleted a slide by mistake, you can get it back by opening the Edit menu and selecting Undo, or by clicking on the Undo button (the button with the counterclockwise arrow on it) in the Standard toolbar.

# Cutting, Copying, and Pasting Slides

In Lesson 20, you will learn how to rearrange slides in Slide Sorter and Outline views. However, you can also use the cut, copy, and paste features to help you create duplicate slides and move slides. To cut (or copy) a slide and paste it in a presentation, perform the following steps:

1. Change to Slide Sorter or Outline view.

2. Select the slide(s) you want to copy or cut.

3. Open the Edit menu, and select Cut or Copy. If you chose Cut, the selected slide(s) are removed from the presentation and placed on the Windows Clipboard. If you chose Copy, the original slides remain in the presentation.

> **Windows Clipboard**   The Windows Clipboard is a temporary holding area for cut or copied items. You can cut or copy items to the Clipboard and then paste them on a slide.

> **Quick Cut or Copy**   To bypass the **E**dit menu, press Ctrl+C to copy or Ctrl+X to cut, or click on the Cut or Copy button in the Standard toolbar.

4. Perform one of the following steps:

   • In Slide Sorter view, select the slide after which you want the cut or copied slide(s) placed.

   • In Outline view, move the insertion point to the end of the text for the slide after which you want the cut or copied slide(s) placed.

5. Open the Edit menu, and choose Paste, or press
   Ctrl+V. (You can also click on the Paste button in
   the Standard toolbar.) The cut or copied slides are
   inserted.

## Dragging and Dropping Slides

A quick way to copy or move a slide is to use the Drag and
Drop feature, as follows:

1. Change to the Slide Sorter or Outline view.

> **Dragging and Dropping Between
> Presentations**   You can drag and drop slides
> from one presentation to another. Use the File
> Open command to open both presentations (see
> Lesson 5). Each presentation is displayed in a separate
> window. Open the Window menu, and select Arrange
> All. The two windows appear side-by-side. Change to
> Slide Sorter view in each window. You can now drag
> and drop slides from one window to the other.

2. Click on the slide you want to move or copy.

3. Move the mouse pointer over the slide you want to
   move or copy.

4. Hold down the mouse button (and the Ctrl key if
   you want to copy), and drag the slide to the desired
   position, as shown in Figure 8.2. (If you don't want
   the Ctrl key, PowerPoint moves the slide rather than
   copying it.)

5. Release the mouse button (and the Ctrl key, if you
   were holding it down).

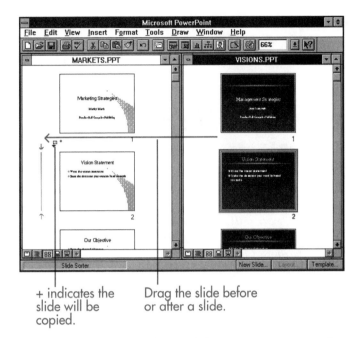

+ indicates the
slide will be
copied.

Drag the slide before
or after a slide.

**Figure 8.2**  You can drag a slide in a presentation or from
one presentation to another.

In this lesson, you learned how to insert, delete, cut,
copy, and paste slides. In the next lesson, you will learn how
to add text objects to slides.

# Lesson

# Adding a Text Object to a Slide

*In this lesson, you will learn how to add text to a slide, change the text alignment and line spacing, and transform text into a bulleted list.*

## Creating a Text Box

If the only text you need in your presentation is the title and a bulleted list, you can add text simply by typing it in Outline or Slide view. However, if you want to type additional text on the slide, you must first create a text box. The text box acts as a receptacle for the text. Text boxes are commonly used for bulleted lists, notes, and labels (used to point to important parts of illustrations). To create a text box, perform the following steps:

1. Click on the Text tool as shown here:

2. Move the mouse pointer to where you want the upper left corner of the box to appear.

3. Hold down the mouse button, and drag the mouse pointer to the right until the box is the desired width.

4. Release the mouse button. A one-line text box appears. (See Figure 9.1.)

Insertion point

**Figure 9.1**   The text box appears with a blinking insertion point inside.

5. Type the text that you want to appear in the text box. When you reach the right side of the box, PowerPoint wraps the text to the next line, and makes the box one line deeper. To start a new paragraph, press Enter.

6. Click anywhere outside the text box.

**Framing a Text Box**   The border that appears around a text box when you create or select it does not appear on the printed slide. To add a border that does print, see Lesson 18.

## Selecting, Deleting, and Moving a Text Box

If you go back and click anywhere inside the text box, a *selection box* appears around it. If you click on the selection box border, handles appear around the text box, as shown in Figure 9.2. You can drag the box's border to move the box, or drag a handle (as shown) to resize it. PowerPoint will wrap the text automatically, as needed to fit inside the box. To delete a text box, select it (so handles appear around it), and then press the Del key.

Handles ——

Drag the border to move the box.

**Figure 9.2** Click on the selection box border to display handles.

## Editing Text in a Text Box

To edit text in a text box, first click anywhere inside the text box to select it. Then, perform any of the following steps:

* **To select text**, drag the I-beam pointer over the text you want to select. (To select a single word, double-click on it. To select an entire sentence, triple-click.)

> **Auto Word Select** When you drag over text, PowerPoint selects whole words. If you want to select individual characters, open the Tools menu, select Options, and select Automatic Word Selection to turn it off. Click on the OK button.

* **To delete text**, select the text and press the Del key. You can also use the Del or Backspace keys to delete single characters.

* **To insert text**, click the I-beam pointer where you want the text inserted, and then type the text.

* **To replace text**, select the text you want to re-place, and then type the new text. When you start typing, the selected text is deleted.

* **To copy and paste text**, select the text you want to copy, and choose the Copy command from the Edit menu, or press Ctrl+C. Move the insertion point to where you want the text pasted (it can be in a different text box), and choose Paste from the Edit menu, or press Ctrl+V.

- **To cut and paste (move) text**, select the text you want to cut, and choose the Cut command from the Edit menu, or press Ctrl+X. Move the insertion point to where you want the text pasted (it can be in a different text box), and choose Paste from the Edit menu, or press Ctrl+V.

## Changing the Text Alignment and Line Spacing

When you first type text, it is set against the left edge of the text box and is single-spaced. To change the paragraph alignment, perform the following steps:

**1.** Click anywhere inside the paragraph whose alignment you want to change.

**2.** Open the Format menu, and select Alignment. The Alignment submenu appears.

**3.** Select **Left**, **Center**, **Right**, or **Justify**, to align the paragraph as desired. (See Figure 9.3 for examples.)

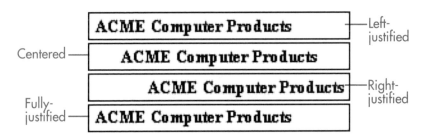

**Figure 9.3**   You can align each paragraph in a text box.

**Quick Alignment**   To quickly set the alignment for a paragraph, click inside the paragraph, and press one of the following key combinations: Ctrl+L for left alignment or Ctrl+R for right alignment. You can center text by clicking on the Center Alignment button in the Formatting toolbar. You can left-justify text by clicking on the Left Alignment button.

To change the line spacing in a paragraph, perform these steps:

**1.** Click inside the paragraph whose line spacing you want to change, or select all the paragraphs whose line spacing you want to change.

**2.** Open the Format menu, and select Line Spacing. The Line Spacing dialog box appears, as shown in Figure 9.4.

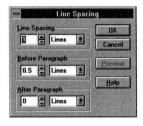

**Figure 9.4**   The Line Spacing dialog box.

**3.** Click on the arrow buttons to the right of any of the following text boxes to change the line spacing:

**L**ine Spacing   This setting controls the space between the lines in a paragraph.

**B**efore Paragraph   This setting controls the space between this paragraph and the paragraph that comes before it.

**A**fter Paragraph   This setting controls the space between this paragraph and the paragraph that comes after it.

**Lines or Points?**   The drop-down list box that appears to the right of each setting allows you to set the line spacing in *lines* or *points*. A line is the current line height (based on text size). A point is a unit commonly used to measure text. A point is approximately 1/72 of an inch.

**4.** Click on the OK button. Your line spacing changes are put into effect.

## Making a Bulleted List

In the next lesson, you will learn the ins and outs of bulleted lists. However, here's a quick lesson on how to turn your text into a bulleted list:

**1.** Click inside the paragraph you want to transform into a bulleted list, or select one or more paragraphs.

**2.** Open the Format menu, and select Bullet. The Bullet dialog box appears.

**3.** Click on Use a Bullet, and then click on the OK button. PowerPoint transforms the selected text into a bulleted list. (If you press Enter at the end of a bulleted paragraph, the next paragraph has a bullet.)

> **Quick Bullets**  To bypass the Format menu and Bullet dialog box, simply click on the Bullet button in the Formatting toolbar. You can click on the Bullet button again to remove the bullet.

## Adding a WordArt Object

PowerPoint 4 comes with an *applet* (tiny application) called WordArt that can help you create graphic text effects. To insert a WordArt object into a slide, perform the following steps:

**1.** Display the slide on which you want the WordArt object placed.

**2.** Open the Insert menu, and select Object. The Insert Object dialog box appears.

**3.** In the Object **Type** list, click on Microsoft WordArt
2.0, and click on the OK button. The Microsoft
WordArt toolbar and text entry box appear, as
shown in Figure 9.5.

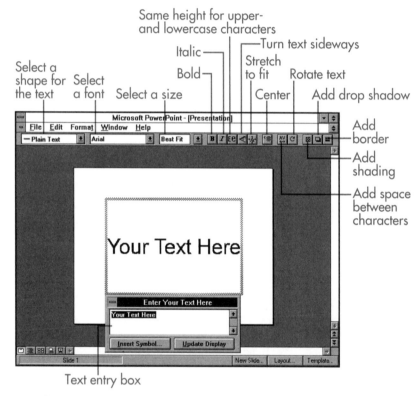

**Figure 9.5** Type your text and use the WordArt toolbar to
style it.

**4.** Type the text you want to use. Whatever you type
replaces the Your Text Here message. (As you type,
press Enter if you need to start a new line.)

**5.** Select a WordArt font from the font list.

**6.** Select a text size from the size list. If you do not specify a size, Word adjusts the text automatically to fit the size of the WordArt box.

**7.** Select a shape from the shape list. Shapes act as cookie cutters, forming the text.

**8.** Use the formatting buttons, as show in Figure 9.5, to create additional effects. (For more formatting options, open the Format menu.)

**9.** Click anywhere inside the presentation window to return to your slide. The WordArt appears on your slide.

To edit the WordArt object at any time, double-click on it to display the WordArt toolbar and text entry box. Enter your changes, and then click outside the WordArt object. You can move the object by dragging its border, or resize it by dragging a handle.

In this lesson, you learned how to add text to a slide, change the text alignment and spacing, transform text into a bulleted list, and add WordArt objects. In the next lesson, you will learn how to use tables, tabs, and indents to create columns and lists.

# Lesson 10

# Creating Columns and Lists

*In this lesson, you will learn how to use tabs to create columns of text and use indents to create bulleted lists, numbered lists, and other types of lists.*

## Using Tabs to Create Columns

A presentation often uses tabbed columns to display information. For example, you may use tabs to create a three-column list like the one shown in Figure 10.1.

**Figure 10.1** You can use tabs to create a multi-column list.

To set the tabs for such a list, perform the following steps:

1. Click anywhere inside the text box for which you want to set the tabs.

2. If you already typed text inside the text box, select the text.

3. Open the View menu, and select Ruler. The ruler appears at the top of the presentation window.

4. Click on the tab icon in the upper left corner of the presentation window until it represents the type of tab you want to set:

> **L** Aligns the left end of the line against the tab stop.

> Centers the text on the tab stop.

> Aligns the right end of the line against the tab stop.

> Aligns the tab stop on a period. This is useful for aligning a column of numbers that use decimal points.

5. Click on each place in the ruler where you want to set the selected type of tab stop, as shown in Figure 10.2.

6. Repeat steps 4 and 5 if you want to set different types of tab stops at different positions.

7. To change the position of an existing tab stop setting, drag it on the ruler to the desired position. To delete an existing tab stop setting, drag it off the ruler.

8. To turn off the ruler, open the View menu, and select Ruler.

**Don't Forget the Slide Master**   Throughout this lesson, keep in mind that you can enter your changes on the slide master or on individual slides. If you change the slide master, the change affects all slides in the presentation. For details on displaying the slide master, see Lesson 7.

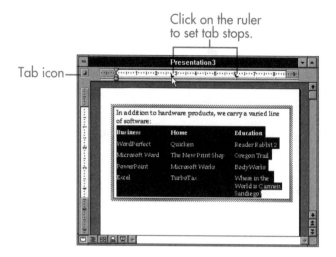

**Figure 10.2**  The ruler lets you enter and change tab stop settings.

## Using Indents to Create Lists

Indents allow you to move one or more lines of a paragraph in from the left margin. PowerPoint uses indents to create the bulleted lists you encountered in Lesson 4. You can use indents in any text object to create a similar list, or your own custom list. To indent text, perform the following steps:

**1.** Select the text box that contains the text you want to indent.

**2.** If you already typed text, select the text you want to indent.

**3.** Open the View menu, and select Ruler. The ruler appears above the text box.

**4.** Drag one of the indent markers (as shown in Figure 10.3) to set the indents for the paragraph:

Drag the top marker to indent the first line.

Drag the bottom marker to indent all subsequent lines.

Drag the box below the bottom marker to indent all the text.

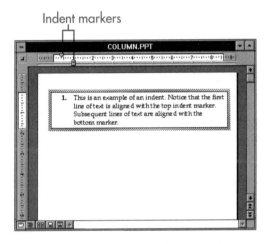

**Figure 10.3**  Drag the indent markers to indent your text.

5. To turn the ruler off, open the View menu, and select Ruler.

You can create up to five levels of indents within a single text box. To add an indent level, click on the Demote button in the Formatting toolbar, or press Alt+Shift+→. A new set of indent markers appears, showing the next level of indents. You can change these new indent settings as explained above.

Once you have set your indents, you can create a numbered or bulleted list by performing the following steps:

1. Type a number and a period, or type the character you want to use for the bullet.

2. Press the Tab key to move to the second indent mark.

3. Type the text you want to use for this item. As you type, the text is wrapped to the second indent mark.

## Changing the Bullet Character

By default, whenever you click on the Bullet button in the Formatting toolbar to insert a bullet, PowerPoint inserts a large dot for the bullet. However, you can change the appearance of the bullet at any time by performing the following steps:

1. Select the paragraph(s) in which you want to change the bullet character.

2. Open the Format menu, and select Bullet. The Bullet dialog box appears.

3. Pull down the Bullets From list, and select the character set from which you want to choose a bullet. The dialog box displays the characters in the selected set.

4. Click on the character you want to use for the bullet.

5. To set the size of the bullet, use the up and down arrows to the right of the Size text box.

6. To select a color for the bullet, pull down the Special Color drop-down list, and select the desired color.

7. Select the OK button. The bullet character is changed for all selected paragraphs.

**Numbered Lists**   PowerPoint offers little help for creating numbered lists. You must type the number for each item yourself.

**Moving a Bulleted Item**   You can move an item in a bulleted list by clicking on the item's bullet and then dragging the bullet up or down in the list.

In this lesson, you learned how to create columns with tabs, create lists with indents, and change the bullet character for bulleted lists. In the next lesson, you will learn how to change the style, size, and color of text.

# Lesson

# Changing the Look of Your Text

*In this lesson, you will learn how to change the appearance of text by changing its font, style, size, and color.*

## Enhancing Your Text with the Font Dialog Box

You can enhance your text by using the Font dialog box or by using various tools on the Formatting toolbar. Use the Font dialog box if you want to add several enhancements to your text at one time. Use the Formatting toolbar to add one enhancement at a time.

**Fonts, Styles, and Effects**   In PowerPoint, a *font* is a family of text that has the same design or *typeface* (for example, Arial or Courier). A *style* is a standard enhancement, such as bold or italic. An *effect* is a special enhancement, such as shadow or underline.

You can change the fonts for existing text or for text you are about to type by performing the following steps:

1. To change the look of existing text, drag the I-beam pointer over the text.

2. Open the Format menu, and select Font. The Font dialog box appears, as shown in Figure 11.1.

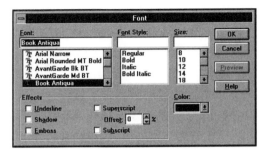

**Figure 11.1** The Font dialog box allows you to select a font.

**3.** From the Font list, select the font you want to use.

> **TrueType Fonts** The TT next to a font name
> marks the font as a TrueType font. TrueType fonts
> are *scalable*, meaning that you can set them at
> any point size. When you save a presentation,
> you can choose to embed TrueType fonts so you
> can display or print the font on any computer whether or
> not it has that font installed.

**4.** From the Font Style list, select any style you want to apply to the type. (Regular removes any styles you may have applied.)

**5.** In the Size text box, type a desired type size, or select a size from the list. (With TrueType fonts, you can type any point size, even sizes that do not appear on the list.)

**6.** In the Effects group, select any special effects you want to add to the text, such as Underline, Shadow, or Emboss.

**7.** To change the color of your text, click on the arrow button to the right of the Color list, and click on the desired color. (For more colors, click on the Other Color option at the bottom of the list, and use the dialog box that appears to select a color.)

**8.** Click on the OK button to apply the new look to your text. (If you selected text before styling it, the text appears in the new style. If you did not select text, any text you type will appear in the new style.)

---

**Title and Object Area Text**   If you change a font on an individual slide, the font is changed only on that slide. To change the font for all the slides in the presentation, change the font on the slide master. To change the Slide Master, open the View menu, select Master, and select Slide Master. Then, perform the steps above to change the look of the text.

---

## Styling Text with the Formatting Toolbar

As shown in Figure 11.2, the Formatting toolbar contains many tools for changing the font, size, style, and color of text.

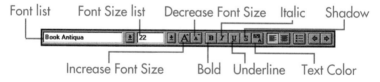

**Figure 11.2**  The Formatting toolbar contains several tools for styling text.

To use the tools, perform the following steps:

**1.** To change the look of existing text, select the text.

**2.** To change fonts, click on the arrow to the right of the Font list, and then click on the desired font.

**3.** To specify a different type size, click inside the Font Size text box and type a size (in points), or click on the arrow to the right of the text box and select a size.

**Incrementing the Type Size**   To increase or decrease the text size to the next size up or down, click on the Increase Font Size or Decrease Font Size button in the Formatting toolbar.

4. To add a style or effect to the text (bold, italic, underline, and/or shadow), click on the appropriate button: **B** for Bold, **I** for Italic, **U** for Underline, or **S** for Shadow.

5. To change the color of the text, click on the Text Color button, and then click on the desired color. (For more colors, click on the Other Color option at the bottom of the list, and use the dialog box that appears to select a color.)

**Watch Those Color Schemes**   The colors listed on the Color menu complement the background colors in the template. If you choose an "other" color, you risk using one that will clash with the background colors and make your slides look inconsistent.

## Copying Text Formats

If your presentation contains text that has the styling you want to use, you can pick up the style from the existing text and apply it to other text. Perform the following steps:

1. Highlight the text whose style you want to use.

2. Open the Format menu, and select Pick Up Text Style. PowerPoint copies the style.

3. Select the text to which you want to apply the style.

4. Open the Format menu, and select Apply Text Style. The selected text takes on the look of the source text.

The text style you picked up remains in a temporary holding area until you pick up another style, so you can continue to apply it to other text.

**Painting Styles**   You can bypass the Format menu by using the Format Painter button in the Standard toolbar. Drag over the text whose style you want to copy, and click on the Format Painter button. Drag over the text to which you want to copy the style. When you release the mouse button, the copied format is applied to the selected text.

In this lesson, you learned how to change the appearance of text by changing its font, size, style, and color. In the next lesson, you will learn how to draw objects on a slide.

# 12

# Drawing Objects on a Slide

*In this lesson, you will learn how to use PowerPoint's drawing tools to draw graphic objects on a slide.*

## PowerPoint's Drawing Tools

You may find it necessary to include basic graphic objects on a slide. For example, you may want to draw a simple logo, or accent your slide with horizontal or vertical lines. PowerPoint comes with several drawing tools that you can use to draw objects on a slide. PowerPoint's drawing tools are displayed along the left side of the presentation window in Slide view and Notes Pages view. (See Figure 12.1).

## Drawing a Line or Shape

The general procedure for drawing an object is the same, no matter which object you draw:

1. Click on the button in the Drawing toolbar for the line or shape you want to draw.

2. Move the mouse pointer to where you want one end of the line or one corner of the object to be anchored.

3. Hold down the mouse button, and drag to where you want the opposite end of the line or corner of the object to appear (see Figure 12.1).

4. Release the mouse button.

Drawing toolbar

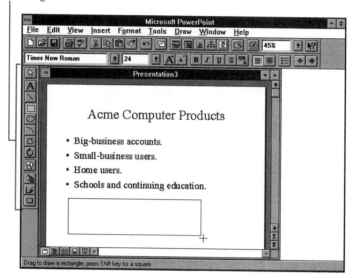

**Figure 12.1** The Drawing toolbar contains tools for drawing lines and basic shapes.

**Drawing Irregular Objects** The previous steps work well for lines, rectangles, and ovals, but if you choose the Freeform tool, you must use some different techniques. To draw freehand, hold down the mouse button, and drag the pointer around on-screen. To create a polygon (an object made up of several straight line segments), click where you want the end point of each line (this works like connect-the-dots). To create a closed shape, click on the original point. To create an open shape, press Esc.

# Tips for Working with Objects

Following is a list of additional drawing tips that can save you some time and reduce frustration:

- To draw several objects of the same shape, double-click on the tool, and then use the mouse to create as many of those shapes as you like.

- To draw a uniform object (a perfect circle or square), hold down the Shift key while dragging.

- To draw an object out from the center rather than from a corner, hold down the Ctrl key while dragging.

- To select an object, click on it.

- To delete an object, select it, and press Del.

- To move an object, select it, and drag one of its lines.

- To resize or reshape an object, select it, and drag one of its handles.

- To copy an object, hold down the Ctrl key while dragging it.

- To quickly change the look of an object, right-click on it, and select the desired option from the shortcut menu.

**Line Thickness, Color, and Shading**
Lesson 18 provides details about how to enhance drawings and other graphic objects by changing the line thickness, color, and shading. However, you can add the enhancements now by opening the Format menu and selecting Colors and Lines. The Colors and Lines dialog box lets you add arrow heads to lines, too.

# Drawing a PowerPoint AutoShape

PowerPoint comes with several predrawn objects, called AutoShapes, that you can add to your slides. To add one of these objects, perform the following steps:

**1.** Click on the AutoShapes tool in the Drawing toolbar. The AutoShapes palette appears, as shown in Figure 12.2.

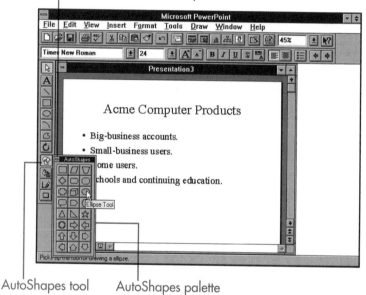

Double-click here to close the palette

AutoShapes tool     AutoShapes palette

**Figure 12.2** Select the desired shape from the AutoShapes palette.

**2.** Click on the shape you want to draw.

**3.** Move the mouse pointer where you want a corner or the center of the shape to be.

4. (Optional) While drawing the object, hold down one or both of the following keys:

Ctrl to draw the shape out from a center point.

Shift to draw a shape that retains the dimensions shown on the AutoShapes palette.

5. Hold down the mouse button, and drag the mouse to draw the object.

6. Release the mouse button.

**Changing an Existing Shape**   You can change an existing shape into a different shape. Select the shape you want to change, open Draw menu, select Change AutoShape, and click on the shape you want to use.

# Rotating an Object

New to PowerPoint is the Free Rotate tool that allows you to spin an object around its center point. To rotate an object, do the following:

1. Click on the object you want to spin.

2. Click on the Free Rotate tool in the Drawing toolbar (this is the button with the clockwise arrow on it).

3. Move the mouse pointer over any of the object's handles.

4. Hold down the mouse button, and drag the handle until the object is in the desired position.

5. Release the mouse button.

**Other Spin Options** The **D**raw menu contains a Rotate/Fli**p** submenu that provides additional rotation options. You can flip an object 90 degrees left or right, or flip the object over an imaginary vertical or horizontal line to create a mirrored image of it.

# Adding Text to an Object

You can add text to a rectangle, oval, or shape, by performing the following steps:

1. Click on the object in which you want the text to appear.

2. Type the text. As you type, the text appears in a single line across the object.

3. Open the Format menu, and select Text Anchor. The Text Anchor dialog box appears, as shown in Figure 12.3.

4. Select one of the following options to have the text included in the object:

   Adjust Object Size to **F**it Text changes the size of the object to fit around the existing text.

   **W**ord-wrap Text in Object wraps the text so it fits inside the object.

**Viewing the Effects of Your Changes** You can drag the title bar of the dialog box to move the dialog box away from the object. That way, you will be able to view the effects of your changes as you work.

**5.** Click on the arrow to the right of the Anchor Point drop-down list, and select an anchor point for the text. For example, if you select Bottom, text will sit on the bottom of the object.

**6.** If desired, use the Box Margins boxes to set the left, right, top, and bottom margins for your text. By increasing the margins, you force the text in toward the center of the object. By decreasing the margins, you allow the text to reach out toward the edges.

**7.** Click on the OK button to save your changes.

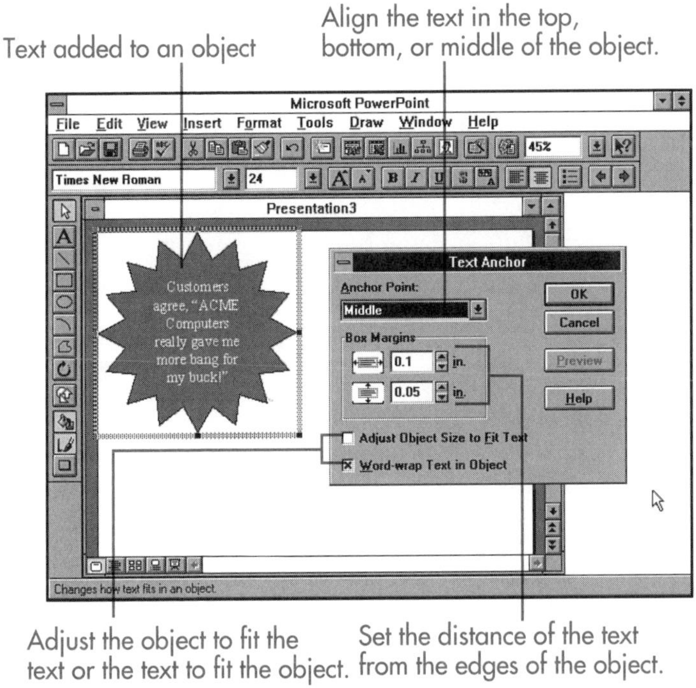

Align the text in the top, bottom, or middle of the object.

Text added to an object

Adjust the object to fit the text or the text to fit the object.

Set the distance of the text from the edges of the object.

**Figure 12.3** Use the Text Anchor dialog box to position your text inside the object.

You can change the style and alignment of the text in an object in the same way you can change style and alignment in any text box. Refer to Lessons 9, 10, and 11 for details.

In this lesson, you learned how to use PowerPoint's drawing tools to add basic shapes and line drawings to your slides. In the next lesson, you will learn how to add PowerPoint clip art objects and recorded sounds to your slides.

# Lesson

# Adding Pictures and Sounds

*In this lesson, you will learn how to add PowerPoint clip art, drawings created in other graphic programs, and recorded sounds to a slide.*

## Adding PowerPoint Clip Art

PowerPoint comes with hundreds of clip art images that you can use in your presentations.

> **Clip Art** Clip art is a collection of previously created images or pictures that you can place on a slide.

To insert a clip art image onto a slide, perform the following steps:

**1.** In Slide view, display the slide on which you want to insert the clip art image.

**2.** Open the Insert menu, and select Clip Art, or click on the Insert Clip Art button in the Standard toolbar. The Microsoft ClipArt Gallery appears, as shown in Figure 13.1.

**First Time?**   If this is the first time you have
selected to insert a clip art image, PowerPoint
displays a dialog box asking for your confirma-
tion and warning that it will take some time. PowerPoint
uses this time to organize the clip art library and prepare
the images for your use.

Select a category.          Use the scroll bar to view more images.

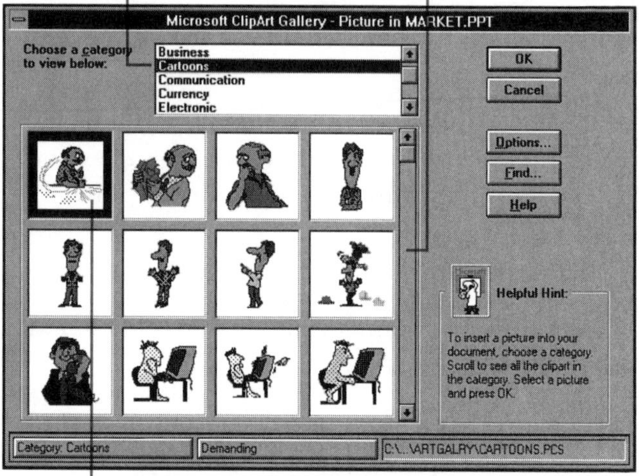

Select a clip art image.

**Figure 13.1**   Select a category and then a clip art image.

3. In the Choose a category list, select the desired
   group of clip art images. PowerPoint displays the
   clip art images that are in the selected category.

4. Click on the desired image. A selection border
   appears around it.

5. Click on the OK button. PowerPoint places the
   selected image on your slide.

6. Move the mouse pointer over the clip art object, hold down the mouse button, and drag the object to the desired position.

**Picture Too Big?**   If the picture is too big or too small, refer to Lesson 17 to learn how to resize and crop (trim) the picture.

## Inserting Pictures Created in Other Applications

In addition to inserting clip art images, PowerPoint allows you to insert pictures created in other graphics programs. To insert a picture, perform the following steps:

1. Open the Insert menu, and select Picture. The Insert Picture dialog box appears, as shown in Figure 13.2.

Select a picture file from the list.

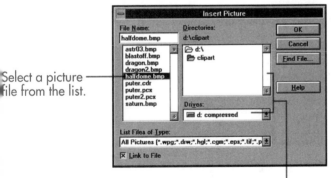

Change to the drive and directory that contains your picture files.

**Figure 13.2**   Use the Insert Picture dialog box to insert a picture created in another program.

2. From the Drives drop-down list, select the drive that contains the desired picture file.

3. From the **Directories** list, change to the directory that contains the file. A list of graphics files appears in the File **Name** list.

4. Click on a file name in the list, or tab to the list and use the ↓ key to highlight a name.

5. To link the graphics file to this slide, select Link to File. If you make this selection, then whenever you change the graphics file using the program you used to create it, the same changes will appear on your PowerPoint slide.

6. Click on the OK button. The picture is inserted on the slide.

7. Move the mouse pointer over the picture, hold down the mouse button, and drag the picture to the desired position.

> **Inserting a New Picture**  If you have a Windows Paint or Draw program, you can insert a picture you have not yet created by opening the Insert menu and selecting **O**bject. Make sure the Create **N**ew option is selected. In the Object **T**ype list, click on the application you need to use to create the picture, and then click on OK. PowerPoint runs the application. After you create your picture and exit the application, PowerPoint inserts the picture on the current slide.

## Changing the Colors of a Picture

When you paste a clip art image or insert a picture on a slide, the picture appears in its original colors. These colors may clash with the colors in your presentation. To change the colors in a picture, perform the following steps:

1. Click on the picture whose colors you want to change. A selection box appears around the picture.

2. Open the Tools menu, and select Recolor. The Recolor Picture dialog box appears, as shown in Figure 13.3.

Select the color you want to change.        Select the color you want to change it to.

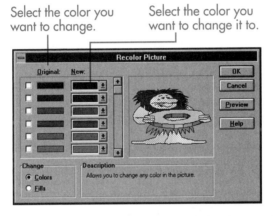

**Figure 13.3** Use the Recolor Picture dialog box to change the colors in a picture.

3. In the Change group, select Colors to change line colors, or Fills to change colors between the lines.

4. Select a color you want to change in the Original list. An X appears in the check box next to the color.

5. Use the New drop-down menu to the right of the selected color to choose the color you want to change to.

**Using the Other Option**    At the bottom of each color's drop-down menu is the **O**ther option. Select this option if you want to use a color that is not listed on the menu.

6. To view the effects of your changes, click on the Preview button.

7. Repeat steps 3 through 6 for each color you want to change.

8. Click on the OK button to put your changes into effect.

## Adding Sounds

If you have sound files (.WAV files) that you recorded on your computer or another computer, or if you have a sound board (such as SoundBlaster Pro) installed on your computer, you can add sounds and music to your presentation. To insert a sound file (.WAV) on a slide, do the following:

1. Display the slide to which you want to apply the sound.

2. Open the Insert menu, and select Object. The Insert Object dialog box appears.

3. In the Object Type list, click on Sound (it's near the bottom of the list).

4. Select Create from File.

> **Recording Sounds**   If you have a sound board installed in your computer, you can choose Create New to record sounds (if you have a microphone, music keyboard, or other input device connected), or you can plug a tape or CD player into the sound board and record music.

**5.** Click on the OK button. The dialog box changes, prompting you to type the path and file name of the sound file you want to use.

**6.** Click on the Browse button, and use the dialog box that appears to select a sound file, and then click on the OK button. This returns you to the Insert Object dialog box. (There are a few .WAV files in the \WINDOWS directory that you can use.)

**7.** Click on the OK button to insert the sound. A small icon appears on the slide to represent the sound.

**8.** Open the Tools menu, and select Play Settings. The Play Settings dialog box appears, as shown in Figure 13.4.

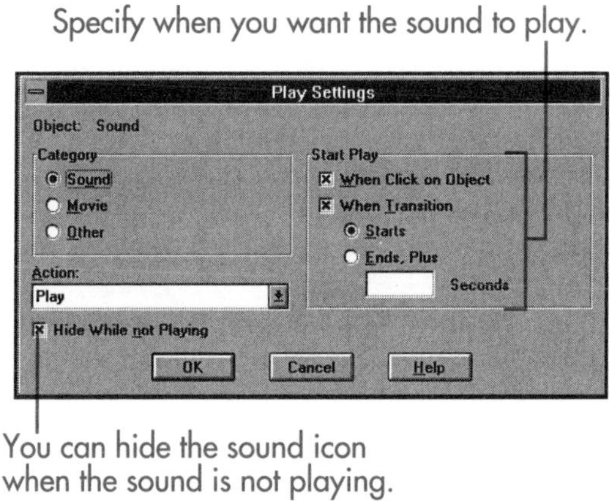

Specify when you want the sound to play.

You can hide the sound icon
when the sound is not playing.

**Figure 13.4** Use the Play Settings dialog box to tell PowerPoint when to play the sound.

**9.** In the Start Play group, specify when you want the sound to play:

When Click on Object tells PowerPoint to play the sound when you click on the object.

When Transition tells PowerPoint to play the sound when the presentation changes from the previous slide to this slide. Starts plays the sound immediately after the previous slide ends. Ends, Plus ____ Seconds plays the sound the specified number of seconds after the transition between slides ends.

**10.** To hide the sound icon when the presentation is not playing the sound, make sure there is an X in the Hide While not Playing check box.

**11.** Click on the OK button.

In this lesson, you learned how to add clip art images, pictures, and sounds to your slides. In the next lesson, you will learn how to add a graph to a slide.

# Lesson

# Adding a Graph
# to a Slide

*In this lesson, you will learn how to create a graph (chart) and place it on a presentation slide.*

## Inserting a Graph

PowerPoint comes with a program called Microsoft Graph that can transform raw data into professional looking graphs. To create a graph, perform the following steps:

1. Display the slide to which you want to add the graph.

2. Click on the Insert Graph button in the Standard toolbar, or open the Insert menu, and choose Microsoft Graph. The Microsoft Graph window appears, as shown in Figure 14.1, with the Datasheet window up front.

 ———— Insert Graph button

**Datasheet** The *Datasheet* is set up like a spreadsheet with rows, columns, and cells. Each rectangle in the Datasheet is a *cell* which can hold text or numbers. Microsoft Graph converts the data you enter into a graph which is displayed in the Graph window.

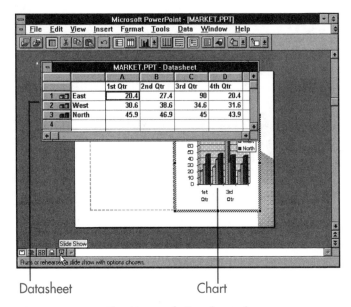

Datasheet                    Chart

**Figure 14.1**  The Microsoft Graph window.

3. Click inside the cell that contains a label or value you want to change, and type your entry.

4. Click on the next cell you want to change, or use the arrow keys to move from cell to cell.

5. Repeat steps 3 and 4 until all your data is entered.

6. Click anywhere inside the graph window. The Datasheet window disappears, and the graph appears.

7. To leave Microsoft Graph and return to your slide in PowerPoint, click anywhere outside the graph.

> **Moving and Resizing the Graph**  If the graph is too big or is poorly positioned on the slide, you can resize and move it. Refer to Lesson 17 for details.

# Editing the Datasheet

If you returned to your slide and later decide that you want
to edit the data that your graph is based on, perform the
following steps to return to Microsoft Graph and display the
Datasheet:

1. Display the slide that contains the graph you want
   to edit.

2. Double-click anywhere inside the graph.
   PowerPoint starts Microsoft Graph and displays the
   graph.

3. If the Datasheet window is not displayed, open the
   View menu, and select Datasheet, or click on the
   View Datasheet button. The Datasheet window
   appears.

4. Tab to the cell that contains the value you want to
   change, and type your change.

5. When you are done, click anywhere inside the
   graph window.

   In addition to editing individual data entries, you can
cut, copy, and paste cells; delete or insert rows and columns;
and adjust the column widths. The following list gives you a
quick overview:

**Selecting Cells**   To select one cell, click on it. To
select several cells, drag the mouse pointer over the
desired cells. To select a row or column, click on the
letter above the column or the number to the left of
the row. To select all the cells, click on the upper-
leftmost square in the Datasheet.

**Clearing Cells**   To erase the contents of cells, select
the cells, and then open the Edit menu, and select
Clear. Select All (to clear contents and formatting),
Contents (to remove only the contents), or Formats
(to remove only the formatting).

**Cutting or Copying Cells**   To cut cells, select the cells you want to cut, and then open the Edit menu, and select Cut, or click on the Cut button in the toolbar. To copy cells, select the cells you want to copy, and then open the Edit menu, and select Copy, or click on the Copy button in the toolbar.

**Pasting Cells**   To paste copied or cut cells into a datasheet, select the cell in the upper left corner of the area in which you want to paste the cut or copied cells. Open the Edit menu, and select Paste, or click on the Paste button in the toolbar.

**Inserting Blank Cells**   To insert blank cells, select the row, column, or number of cells you want to insert. (Rows will be inserted above the current row. Columns will inserted to the left of the current column.) Open the Insert menu, and select Cells. If you selected a row or column, the row or column is inserted. If you selected one or more cells, the Insert Cells dialog box appears, asking if you want to shift surrounding cells down or to the right. Select your preference, and then click on the OK button.

**Changing the Column Width**   If you typed entries that are too wide for a particular column, you may want to adjust the column width. Move the mouse pointer over the column letter at the top of the column whose width you want to change. Move the mouse pointer to the right until it turns into a double-headed arrow. Hold down the mouse button, and drag the mouse until the column is the desired width.

## Changing the Data Series

Say you create a graph that shows the sales figures for several sales persons over four quarters. You wanted each column in the graph to represent a salesperson, but instead, the columns represented quarters. To fix the graph, you can swap the data series by performing the following steps:

**1.** Open the Data menu.

**2.** Select Series in Rows or Series in Columns.

> **Quick Data Series Swap**   To quickly swap data series, click on the By Row or By Column button in the Standard toolbar.

## Changing the Graph Type

By default, Microsoft Graph creates a 3-dimensional column graph. If you want your data displayed in a different type of graph, perform the following steps:

**1.** Open the Format menu, and select Chart Type. The Chart Type dialog box appears, as shown in Figure 14.2.

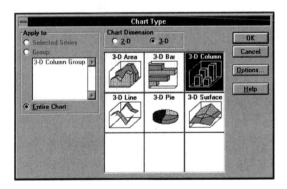

**Figure 14.2**   Pick the desired chart.

**2.** In the Apply to group, make sure Entire Chart is selected.

**3.** In the Chart Dimension group, select 2-D or 3-D. The available graphs for the selected group appear.

**4.** Click on the desired chart type.

**5.** Click on the OK button.

## Selecting a Chart Design with AutoFormat

Microsoft Graph comes with several predesigned chart formats that you can apply to your chart. You simply select the design, and Microsoft Graph reformats your chart, giving it a professional look. Here's how you use AutoFormat to select a chart design:

**1.** Open the Format menu, and choose AutoFormat. The AutoFormat dialog box appears, as shown in Figure 14.3.

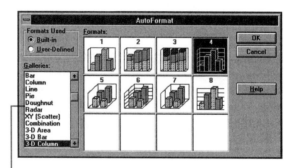

Select a category to view the formats in that category.

**Figure 14.3** Select a chart design from the AutoFormat dialog box.

**2.** From the **G**alleries list, choose a chart type. In the **F**ormats list, Excel shows the available formats for the selected chart type.

**3.** Select the desired chart type from the **F**ormats list.

**4.** Click on the OK button. Excel reformats the chart, using the selected format.

In this lesson, you learned how to create a graph, enter and edit data, and add the graph to a slide. In the next lesson, you will learn how to enhance the graph.

# Lesson

# Enhancing Charts

*In this lesson, you will learn how to enhance your charts to display data more clearly and more attractively.*

## What Can You Add to a Chart?

You can format existing elements and add elements to a chart to enhance it. Following is a list of some of the more common enhancements:

**Fonts**   You can specify a type style, size, and attributes for the text used in the chart.

**Colors**   You can change the color of text or of the lines, bars, and pie slices that are used to represent data.

**Titles and Labels**   You can add a title to the chart or add labels for any of the axes.

**Axes**   You can display or hide the lines used for the X and Y axes.

**Text Boxes**   You can add explanatory text or other text in a separate box.

**Borders and Shading**   You can add a border around a chart or add background shading.

# Displaying the Chart in Microsoft Graph

Before you can enhance an existing chart, you must display it in Microsoft Graph. Perform the following steps:

**1.** In Slide view, display the slide that contains the graph you want to enhance.

**2.** Click on the graph to select it. A selection box appears around the graph.

**3.** Open the Edit menu, and select Chart Object. The Chart Object submenu appears.

**4.** Select Edit. PowerPoint starts Microsoft Graph and displays the graph.

**Double-Click on the Graph**   A quick way to display a graph in Microsoft Graph is to double-click on the graph.

**Text Boxes and Lines**   You can add text boxes, lines, arrows, and basic shapes to graphs in much the same way you can add them to slides. To display the Drawing toolbar for graphs, click on the Drawing button in the Standard toolbar, or right-click on the Standard toolbar and select Drawing. Refer to Lessons 9 and 13 for details on how to use the toolbar buttons to add text boxes, lines, and other shapes.

# Parts of a Chart

Before you start adding enhancements to a chart, you should understand that a chart is made up of several objects. By clicking on an object, you make it active, and handles appear around it, as shown in Figure 15.1. You can then move or resize the object or change its appearance, by doing any of the following:

- Double-click on an object to display a dialog box that lets you change the object's appearance. For example, if you double-click on a column in a column chart, you can change its color.

- Right-click on the object, and then select the desired formatting option from the shortcut menu.

- Select the object, and then select an option from the **Insert** or **Format** menu. The **Insert** menu lets you add objects to a chart, including a legend, data labels, and a chart title.

The following sections tell you how to add some more commonly used enhancements to a chart.

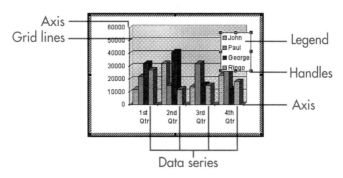

**Figure 15.1**    Each chart consists of several individual objects.

## Adding a Title

You can add various titles to a chart to help indicate what the chart is all about. You can add a chart title that appears at the top of the chart, and you can add axis titles that appear along the X and Y axes. Here's how you do it:

1. Right-click on the chart, and choose Insert Titles, or open the Insert menu and choose Titles.

2. Click on each title type you want to add, to put an X in their check boxes.

3. Click on the OK button. Microsoft Graph returns you to the chart window and inserts text boxes for each title.

4. Click on a text box to select it, click inside the text box, and then edit the text as desired.

## Formatting Text on a Chart

Any text you add to a chart is added inside a text box. To format text you added, do this:

1. Right-click on the text that you want to format. A text box appears around the text, and a shortcut menu appears.

2. Select the Format option. The Format option differs depending on the object. If you right-click on the chart title, the option reads Format Chart Title.

3. Enter your preferences in the Format dialog box. This dialog box typically contains tabs for changing the font, adding borders and shading to the text box, and changing the alignment of text in the box, but you may get only the Font tab.

4. Click on OK when you are done.

## Formatting the Axes

You can enhance the X and Y axes in a number of ways, including changing the font of the text, scaling the axes, and changing the number format. Here's how you do it:

1. Right-click on the axis you want to format, and choose Format Axis, or click on the axis, open the Format menu, and choose Selected Axis. The Format Axis dialog box appears, as shown in Figure 15.2.

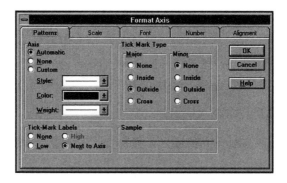

**Figure 15.2** The Format Axis dialog box lets you change the look of the axis and its text.

2. Enter your preferences in the dialog box.

3. Click on OK, or press Enter.

## Enhancing the Chart Frame

You can change the overall look of a chart by adding a border or shading. Perform the following steps:

1. Click on the chart anywhere outside a specific chart object. Handles appear around the entire chart.

**2.** Open the Format menu, and choose Selected Chart Area, or right-click on the chart and choose Format Chart Area. The Format Chart Area dialog box appears.

**3.** Enter your border and color preferences, and then click on the OK button.

## Changing the Look of 3-D Charts

3-D charts are commonly used to illustrate volume. In order to make the various 3-Dimensional elements stand out, you may want to tilt the chart or rotate it. Here's how you do it:

**1.** Open the Format menu and choose 3-D View, or right-click on the chart and choose 3-D View. The Format 3-D View dialog box appears, as shown in Figure 15.3. As you make changes, they are reflected in the wire-frame picture in the middle of the 3-D View dialog box.

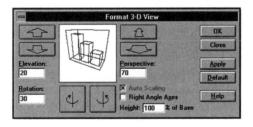

**Figure 15.3**   Changing the 3-D view.

**2.** To change the elevation (height from which the chart is seen), click on the up or down elevation controls, or type a number in the Elevation box.

**3.** To change the rotation (rotation around the Z-axis), click on the left or right rotation controls, or type a number in the Rotation box.

4. If there is a perspective option, you can change the perspective (perceived depth) by clicking on the up or down perspective controls, or typing a number in the **P**erspective box.

5. To see the proposed changes applied to the actual chart, click on the Apply button.

6. When you are done making changes, click on OK, or press Enter.

In this lesson, you learned how to improve the appearance of your chart. In the next lesson, you will learn how to add an organizational chart to a slide.

# Lesson 16

# Adding an Organizational Chart

*In this lesson, you will learn how to add an organizational chart to a slide and how to edit the chart.*

## Inserting an Organizational Chart

PowerPoint comes with a program called Microsoft Organization Chart that can create organizational charts to show the management structure in a company. To create and place an organizational chart on a slide, perform the following steps:

1. Display the slide on which you want the organizational chart placed.

2. Open the Insert menu, and select Object. The Insert Object dialog box appears.

3. In the Object Type list, click on Microsoft Organization Chart 1.0, and click on the OK button. The Microsoft Organization Chart window appears, as shown in Figure 16.1.

Insert Org Chart button    Maximize button

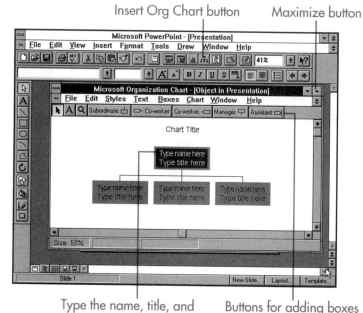

Type the name, title, and        Buttons for adding boxes
up to two comments.

**Figure 16.1**  Type your entries into the basic structure to
form a chart.

> **The Insert Org Chart Button**  To bypass
> the Insert menu, click on the Insert Org Chart
> button in the Standard toolbar.

**4.** If the Organization Chart window is small, click on
the Maximize button in the upper right corner of
the window to make it full-screen size.

**5.** Type the name, title, and up to two optional comments about the person in the organization. Press
Enter after typing each item.

**6.** Press Esc when you are done.

**7.** Click on the next box, or use the arrow keys to

move to the next box. (The up and down arrow keys move up or down a level in the chart. The left and right arrow keys move to the left or right box on the same level.)

**8.** Repeat steps 5–7 for each person you want to include in the organizational chart.

**9.** To add boxes to the chart, click on the appropriate button at the top of the screen, and then click on the box to which you want the new box connected.

**10.** To return to your slide and insert the organizational chart on it, open the File menu, select Exit and Return to, and then click on the Yes button.

# Editing an Organizational Chart

Before you can edit an existing organizational chart, you must display it in Microsoft Organization Chart. Perform the following steps:

**1.** In Slide view, display the slide that contains the organizational chart you want to edit.

**2.** Click on the chart to select it. A selection box appears around the chart.

**3.** Open the Edit menu, and select Microsoft Organization Chart 1.0 Object.

**4.** Select Edit. PowerPoint starts Microsoft Organization Chart and displays the chart.

> **Double-Click on the Chart**   A quick way to display a chart in Microsoft Organization Chart is to double-click on the chart.

As you work on the chart, you can enlarge it or shrink it in the window to view the whole chart or just a portion of it. Open the Chart menu, and select the desired chart size.

## Selecting One or More Levels

As you are editing, adding to, or enhancing an organizational chart, you will need to select the boxes you want to work with. The following list explains how to select one or more boxes or levels:

- To select a single box, click on it. To move from one box to another, use the arrow keys.

- To select more than one box, hold down the Shift key while clicking on each box.

- To select a specific group of boxes (for example, all manager boxes), open the Edit menu, choose Select, and click on the desired group.

- To select a specific level in the organization, open the Edit menu, choose Select Levels, and type the range of levels you would like to select (for example, 2 through 5).

## Cutting, Copying, and Pasting Boxes

To rearrange your organizational chart, you can cut, copy, and paste boxes. Perform the following steps:

**1.** Select the box(es) you want to copy or move.

**2.** Open the Edit menu, and select Cut (to remove the boxes), or Copy (to copy them).

**3.** Select the box to which you want the copied or cut boxes attached.

**4.** Open the Edit menu, and select Paste Boxes. The boxes are pasted to the right of or below the selected box.

**Undoing Cut or Paste**  You can undo any
operation immediately after performing it by
opening the **E**dit menu and selecting **U**ndo. If you
performed two actions, however, you can undo
only the most recent one.

## Selecting a Chart Style

The chart you create resembles a family tree. If that structure
does not suit your needs (for all or part of the chart), you can
change the structure. Perform the following steps:

**1.** Select the boxes to which you want to apply the
new style. To apply your changes to the entire
chart, select all the boxes.

**2.** Open the Styles menu, and click on the desired
style (see Figure 16.2). Organization Chart applies
the specified style to the selected boxes.

Select a structure for part or all of the chart.

**Figure 16.2**  Use the Styles menu to restructure your chart.

## Styling the Text

You may want to use a different font, type style, type size, or color for a person's name and position, or for different levels in the chart. Or you may want to change the text alignment in the box from center to left or right. To style the text in a box, do the following:

**1.** Select the text you want to format:

- Click on a box to format all the text in the box.

- To format part of the text in a box, drag over the desired text.

- Hold down the Shift key, and click on two or more boxes to format the text in every selected box.

**2.** Open the Text menu, and select Font. The Font dialog box appears.

**3.** Change one or more of the following options:

**Font** Select a typeface from the Font list.

**Font Style** Select a style (for example, bold or italic) from the Font Style list.

**Size** Select a type size (in points) from the Size list.

**4.** Click on the OK button.

**5.** To change the color of the text, open the Text menu, select Color, and click on the desired color.

**6.** To change the alignment of the text in the box (from centered to left or right), open the Text menu, and select the desired alignment.

# Changing the Look of the Boxes and Lines

The boxes and lines that make up an organizational chart are formatted for you. However, if you want to change the line or box color or line thickness, or if you want to add a drop shadow to the boxes, perform the following steps:

1.  Select the boxes or lines you want to format. (You can select lines by clicking on them.)

2.  Open the Boxes menu, and select the desired option. A submenu opens, providing you with a list of available settings.

3.  Click on the color, style, or shading you want to use for the selected lines or boxes. Organization Chart applies the selected setting to your organizational chart.

> **Returning to Your Slide**   When you are done editing and enhancing your organizational chart, you can return to your slide by opening the File menu and selecting Exit and Return to. Click on the Yes button to save your changes.

In this lesson, you learned how to create, edit, and enhance an organizational chart. In the next lesson, you will learn how to work with the objects (graphs, organizational charts, text boxes, and drawn objects), which you have placed on a slide.

# Lesson

# Positioning and Sizing Objects

*In this lesson, you will learn how to cut, copy, paste, move, and resize objects on a slide.*

As you may have already discovered, *objects* are the building blocks you use to create slides in PowerPoint. Objects are the shapes you draw, the graphs you create, the pictures you import, and the text you type. In this and the next lesson, you will learn how to manipulate objects on your slides for impressive presentations.

## Selecting Objects

Before you can copy, move, or resize an object, you must first select the object. Change to Slide view, and perform one of the following steps to choose one or more objects:

- To select a single object, click on it. (If you clicked on text, a frame appears around the text. Click on the frame to select the object.)

- To select more than one object, hold down the Shift key while clicking on each object. Handles appear around the selected objects, as shown in Figure 17.1.

- To deselect selected objects, click anywhere outside the selected objects.

**Using the Selection Tool**   The Selection Tool
in the Drawing toolbar (the button with the mouse
pointer on it), allows you to quickly select a group
of objects. Click on the Selection tool, and then use
the mouse pointer to drag a selection box around the
objects you want to select. When you release the mouse
button, the objects inside the box are selected.

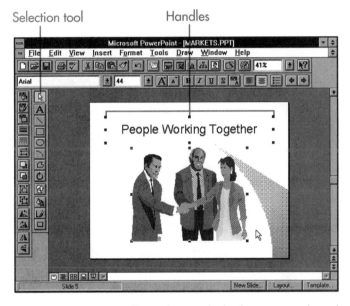

Selection tool                    Handles

**Figure 17.1**   Handles indicate which objects are selected.

## Working with Layers of Objects

As you place objects on-screen, they may start to overlap,
making it difficult or impossible to select the objects in the
lower layers. To relayer objects, perform the following steps:

1. Click on the object you want to move up or down
   in the stack.

2. Open the Draw menu.

**3.** Select one of the following options:

Bring to Front brings the object to the top of the stack.

Send to Back sends the object to the bottom of the stack.

Bring Forward brings the object up one layer.

Send Backward sends the object back one layer.

## Grouping and Ungrouping Objects

Each object you draw acts as an individual object. However, sometimes you'll want two or more objects to act as a group. For example, you may want to make the lines of several objects the same thickness, or move the objects together. If you want two or more objects to always be treated as a group, perform the following steps:

**1.** Select the objects you want to group.

**2.** Open the Draw menu and select Group.

**3.** To ungroup the objects later, select any object in the group, open the Draw menu, and select Ungroup.

**Drawing + Toolbar**   For quick access to the Group, Ungroup, and layering commands, turn on the Drawing + toolbar. Right-click on any toolbar, and then click on Drawing +.

## Cutting, Copying, and Pasting Objects

You can cut, copy, and paste objects on a slide to rearrange the objects or to use the objects to create a picture.

Whenever you cut an object, the object is removed from the slide and placed in a temporary holding area called the Windows Clipboard. When you copy an object, the original object remains on the slide, and a copy of it is placed on the Clipboard. In either case, you can then paste the object from the Clipboard onto the current slide or another slide. Perform the following steps:

**1.** Select the object(s) you want to cut, copy, or move.

**2.** Open the Edit menu, and select Cut or Copy.

> **Quick Cut and Copy**   To quickly cut or copy a selected object, click on the Cut or Copy button in the Standard toolbar, or press Ctrl+X to cut or Ctrl+C to copy.

**3.** Display the slide on which you want the cut or copied object(s) placed.

**4.** Open the Edit menu, and select Paste, or click on the Paste button in the Standard toolbar. The object(s) is pasted on the slide.

**5.** Move the mouse pointer over any of the pasted objects, hold down the mouse button, and drag the objects to where you want them.

**6.** Release the mouse button.

> **Deleting an Object**   To remove an object without placing it on the Clipboard, select the object and then press Del, or open the Edit menu and select Clear.

**Dragging and Dropping Objects**   The quickest way to copy or move objects is to drag and drop them. Select the objects you want to move, position the mouse pointer over any of the selected objects, hold down the mouse button, and drag the objects where you want them. To copy the objects, hold down the Ctrl key while dragging.

## Resizing Objects

There may be times when an object you have created or imported is not the right size for your slide presentation. Resize the object by performing these steps:

1. Select the object to resize.

2. Drag one of the *handles* (the black squares that surround the object) until the object is the desired size:

   • Drag a corner handle to change both the height and width. PowerPoint retains the object's relative dimensions.

   • Drag a side, top, or bottom handle to change the height or width alone.

   • Hold down the Ctrl key while dragging to resize from the center of the picture.

3. Release the mouse button, and the object will be resized (see Figure 17.2).

Drag a handle to resize the object.

**Figure 17.2**  Before and after resizing an object.

## Cropping a Picture

In addition to resizing a picture, you can crop it. That is, you can trim a side or corner of the picture to remove an element from the picture or cut off some white space. To crop a picture, perform the following steps:

**1.** Click on the picture you want to crop.

**2.** Open the Tools menu, and select Crop Picture. The mouse pointer turns into a cropping tool. (See Figure 17.3.)

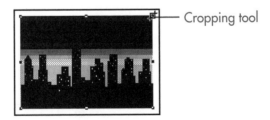

Cropping tool

**Figure 17.3**  Use the cropping tool to chop off a section of the picture.

**3.** Move the mouse pointer over one of the handles. (Use a corner handle to crop two sides at once. Use a side, top, or bottom handle to crop only one side.)

**4.** Hold down the mouse button, and drag the pointer until the crop lines are where you want them.

**5.** Release the mouse button. The cropped section disappears.

> **Uncropping**  You can uncrop a picture immediately after cropping it by opening the **E**dit menu and selecting **U**ndo, or clicking the Undo button on the Standard toolbar. You can uncrop at any time, by performing the steps above and dragging the selected handle in the opposite direction you dragged it for cropping.

In this lesson, you learned how to select, edit, move, and resize an object in a slide. In the next lesson, you will learn how to change the look of an object.

# Lesson 18

# Changing the Look of Objects

*In this lesson, you will learn how to add borders, colors, patterns, and shadows to objects.*

## Framing an Object

You can frame an object by adding a line around the object. To add a line, perform the following steps:

1. Select the object you want to frame.

2. Open the Format menu, and select Colors and Lines. The Colors and Lines dialog box appears, as shown in Figure 18.1.

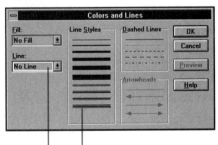

Select a line color.    Select a line thickness or style.

**Figure 18.1**   The Colors and Lines dialog box.

3. Click on the arrow to the right of the **Line** option, and then click on the desired color for the line.

**4.** In the Line Styles list, click on the thickness of the line you want to use.

**5.** Click on the OK button.

> **Instant Thin Line**   To quickly add a thin border around an object, click on the object, and then click on the Apply Line Defaults button in the Drawing toolbar. It's the button with the paintbrush on it.

## Adding a Fill

A *fill* is a background color and shading combination that you can add to an object to make the object stand out. To add a fill or change an existing fill, perform these steps:

**1.** Select the object(s) you want to fill.

**2.** Open the Tools menu, and choose Recolor. The Recolor Picture dialog box appears, as shown in Figure 18.2.

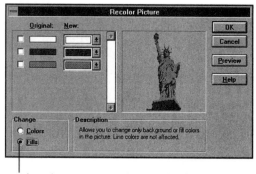

Select this option to change the fill colors.

**Figure 18.2**   You can change each fill color.

**3.** Click on the Fills option. The displayed colors change to show the fill colors.

**4.** Select a color you want to change in the Original list. An X appears in the check box next to the color.

**5.** Use the New drop-down menu to the right of the selected color to choose the color you want to change to.

> **Using the Other Option**   At the bottom of each color's drop-down menu is the **O**ther option. Select this option if you want to use a color that is not listed on the menu.

**6.** To view the effects of your changes, click on the Preview button.

**7.** Repeat steps 3 through 5 for each color you want to change.

**8.** Click on the OK button to put your changes into effect.

> **Quick Fills**   To quickly apply the default fill colors, select the object, and then click on the Apply Fill Defaults button (the button with the paint can on it) in the Drawing toolbar. To remove a fill, select the object, and click on the Apply Fill Defaults button again.

# Adding a Shadow

Adding a shadow gives a 3-D effect to an object, as shown in Figure 18.3. To add a shadow, perform these steps:

Original object ——————— Shadow

**Figure 18.3** The Statue of Liberty with a shadow added.

**1.** Select the object to add a shadow to.

**2.** Open the Format menu, and select Shadow. The Shadow dialog box appears.

**3.** Click on the arrow to the right of the **Color** option, and click on the desired color for the shadow.

**4.** To change the position and thickness of the shadow, enter your settings in the Offset group.

> **Offset** To understand the offset options, think of the shadow as a silhouette of the original object that sits behind the object. You can move the silhouette behind the object in any direction, and move it out more from the object to make the shadow appear thicker.

**5.** Click on the OK button. PowerPoint applies the shadow to the object.

To remove the shadow, repeat the steps above, but select No Shadow from the **Color** drop-down list. You can also remove a shadow by selecting the object and then clicking on the Apply Shadow Defaults button in the Drawing toolbar.

# Copying the Look of Another Object

If your presentation contains an object that has the frame, fill, and shadow you want to use for another object, you can pick up those design elements and apply them to another object. Perform the following steps:

**1.** Click on the object whose style you want to copy.

**2.** Open the Format menu, and select Pick Up Object Style. PowerPoint copies the style.

**3.** Click on the object to which you want to apply the style.

**4.** Open the Format menu, and select Apply Object Style. The selected object takes on the look of the source object.

The style you picked up remains in a temporary holding area until you pick up another style, so you can continue to apply it to other objects.

> **Painting Styles**   You can bypass the Format menu by using the Format Painter button in the Standard toolbar. Select the object whose style you want to copy, and click on the Format Painter button. Select the object to which you want to copy the style.

In this lesson, you learned how to change the look of individual objects on a slide. In the next lesson, you will learn how to change the background colors and designs that appear on every slide in the presentation.

# Lesson

# Working with Colors and Backgrounds

*In this lesson, you will learn how to change the color scheme and background design for a presentation.*

## Understanding Color Schemes and Backgrounds

*Color schemes* are sets of professionally selected complementary colors designed to be used as the primary colors in a presentation. Each color scheme controls the color of the background, lines, text, shadows, fills, and other items on a slide. Using one of these color schemes ensures that your presentation will look appealing and professional.

*Backgrounds* are designs that control the way the color is used on a slide. For example, you can select a background that spreads the color out from the upper left corner to the edges.

You can select a color scheme and background for the master slide (which controls all the slides in the presentation), for the current slide, or for all slides in the presentation (thus overriding the master slide). The following sections explain how to select and manipulate color schemes and backgrounds.

# Selecting a Color Scheme

You can select a color scheme for one slide or for all the slides in your presentation. Perform the following steps:

**1.** Display or select the slide whose color scheme you want to change.

> **Stay Consistent**   Be careful when selecting a color scheme for a single slide in the presentation. You don't want one slide to clash with the rest of your slides. As you will see later, you can apply the new color scheme to one or all of the slides in your presentation.

**2.** Open the Format menu, and select Slide Color Scheme. The Slide Color Scheme dialog box appears.

**3.** Click on the Choose Scheme button. The Choose Scheme dialog box appears.

**4.** From the **B**ackground Color list, select the color you want to use for the slide background. A list of complementary colors appears in the **T**ext & Line Color list.

**5.** From the **T**ext & Line Color list, select a color you want to use for the text and lines on a slide. A selection of samples appears in the **O**ther Scheme Colors group, as shown in Figure 19.1.

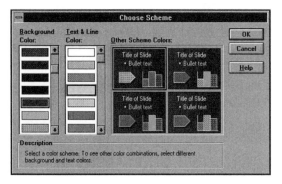

**Figure 19.1** Select a background color, text color, and other colors option.

**6.** From the **O**ther Scheme Colors group, click on the desired look you want for your slides.

**7.** Click on OK when finished selecting colors. You are returned to the Slide Color Scheme dialog box.

**8.** Click on the Apply button to apply the new color scheme only to this slide, or click on Apply to All to apply the color scheme to all the slides in the presentation.

## Changing a Color in the Color Scheme

You can modify any color in a color scheme to create your own custom combinations. For example, you can create a color scheme that matches your company colors or logo. To change a color in a color scheme, perform the following steps:

**1.** Display or select the slide whose color scheme you want to change.

**2.** Open the Format menu, and select Slide Color Scheme. The Slide Color Scheme dialog box appears.

**3.** Click on a color you want to change. (Colors are labeled to show the corresponding items they control.)

**4.** Click on the Change Color button. The Color dialog box for the selected item appears, as shown in Figure 19.2.

Select the item whose color you want to change.

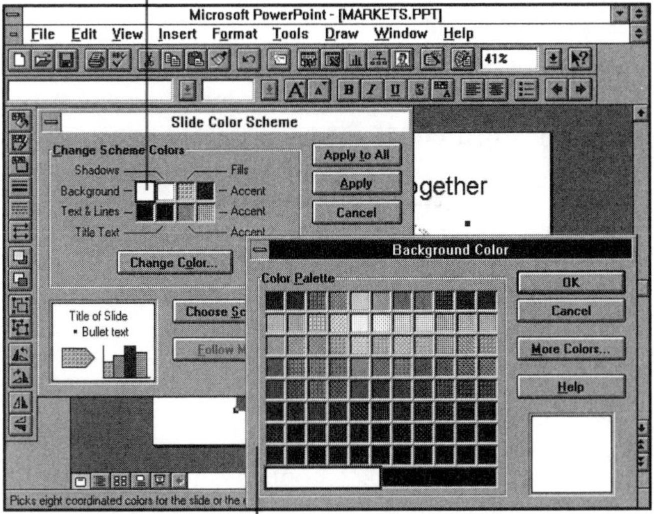

The Change Color button brings up this dialog box.

**Figure 19.2** You can change colors for various items in your presentation.

**5.** Click on the color you want to use.

**Custom Colors**   To create a custom color, click on the More Colors button, and adjust the Hue, Saturation, and Luminance, to create the desired color.

**6.** Click on the OK button to change the color and return to the Color Scheme dialog box.

**7.** Repeat steps 3 through 6 to change any other colors.

**8.** When finished changing colors, click on the Apply or Apply To All button.

## Copying and Applying a Color Scheme to Other Presentations

You can reuse a color scheme you have created in a presentation by copying it and applying it to another presentation. This is particularly useful if you have created a custom color scheme. To copy a color scheme from one presentation to another, do the following:

**1.** Open the presentation that contains the color scheme you want to copy. (See Lesson 5.)

**2.** Open the View menu, and select Slide Sorter, or click on the Slide Sorter button at the bottom of the presentation window.

**3.** Click on the slide which contains the color scheme you want to copy.

**4.** Open the Format menu, and select Pick up Color Scheme.

**5.** Open the presentation to which you want to apply the copied color scheme.

6. Open the View menu, and select Slide Sorter, or click on the Slide Sorter button at the bottom of the presentation window.

7. Select the slide(s) to which you want to apply the copied color scheme. (To select more than one slide, hold down the Shift key while clicking on the slides.)

8. Open the Format menu, and select Apply Color Scheme.

## Changing the Background Design

An effective background can add a professional look to any presentation. To change the background for your presentation or modify the existing background, perform the following steps:

1. Display or select the slide whose background you want to change. (You will be able to apply the background changes to all the slides in the presentation.)

2. Open the Format menu, and select Slide Background. The Slide Background dialog box appears, as shown in Figure 19.3.

3. In the Shade Styles group, select the way you want the background color to fade across the slide. (For example, if you choose From Corner, the color appears pale in one corner and then intensifies as it reaches the edges of the slide.)

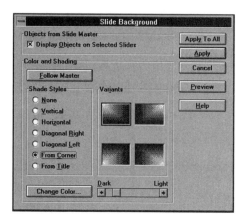

**Figure 19.3** The Slide Background dialog box lets you control the background color and shading.

**4.** To change the background color, click on the Change Color button, click on the color you want to use, and then click on OK. (You can change the background color here or in the Color Scheme, as explained earlier.)

**5.** To change the intensity of the color, use the Dark/ Light slide control.

**6.** In the Variants group, select the desired variation you want to use for the shade style.

**7.** Click on the Apply button to apply the background only to this slide, or click on Apply To All to apply the background to all the slides in the presentation.

In this lesson, you learned how to select and modify a color scheme, and how to copy a color scheme from one presentation to other presentations. You also learned how to change the background color and design for a slide or presentation. In the next lesson, you will learn how to rearrange the slides in a presentation.

# Lesson

# Rearranging Slides

*In this lesson, you will learn how to rearrange your slides in the presentation.*

There may be times when you will need to change the sequence of slides you have created in the presentation. In PowerPoint, you are given the ability to reorder the slides in either Slide Sorter view or Outline view.

## Rearranging in Slide Sorter View

Slide Sorter view shows miniature versions of the slides in your presentation. This allows you to view many of your slides at one time. To rearrange the slides in Slide Sorter view, perform the following steps:

1. Open the View menu, and select Slide Sorter, or click on the Slide Sorter view button, as shown here:

2. Move the mouse pointer over the slide you want to move to a new location.

3. Hold down the mouse button, and drag the mouse pointer over the slide before or after which you want the slide moved. As you drag the mouse pointer, a line appears (as shown in Figure 20.1), showing where the slide will be moved.

4. Release the mouse button. The slide is moved to its new position, and the surrounding slides are shifted to make room for it.

Mouse pointer    Line shows new position of slide.

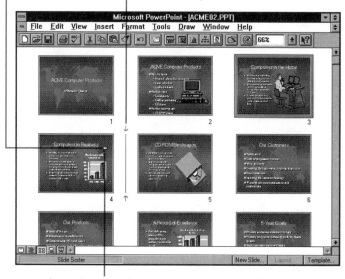

Drag to the right side of the slide to insert after the slide, or to the left side to insert before the slide.

**Figure 20.1** Drag the slide to its new position.

**Copying a Slide** You can copy a slide in Slide Sorter view as easily as you can move a slide. Simply hold down the Ctrl key while dragging.

## Rearranging in Outline View

In Outline view, you can see the titles and text on each slide, giving you a clear picture of the content and organization of your presentation. Because of this, you may prefer to rearrange your slides in Outline view. Here's how you do it:

**1.** Open the View menu, and select Outline, or click on the Outline view button, as shown here:

**2.** Click on the slide number or slide icon to the left of the slide you want to move. The entire slide contents are highlighted.

> **Moving the Contents of a Slide**   You don't have to move an entire slide in the presentation. You can move only the slide's data—from one slide to another—by selecting only what you want to move and dragging it to its new location.

**3.** Move the mouse pointer over the selected slide icon, hold down the mouse button, and drag the slide up or down in the outline, or click on the Move Up or Move Down buttons in the Outlining toolbar as shown in Figure 20.2.

Move up    You can drag the icon up or down.

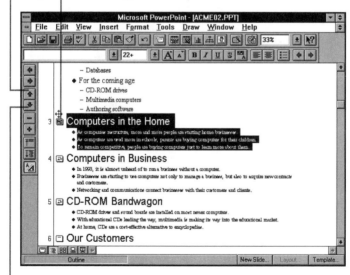

Move down

**Figure 20.2**   Drag the selected icon, or click on the Move Up or Move Down button.

**Collapsing the Outline**   You can *collapse* the outline to show only the slide titles. This allows you to see more slides at one time and rearrange the slides more easily. To collapse the outline, click on the Show Titles button in the Outlining toolbar. To restore the outline, click on the Show All button.

# Hiding Slides

Before you give a presentation, you should try to anticipate any questions from your audience and be prepared to answer those questions. You may even want to create slides to support your answers and then keep the slides hidden until you need them. To hide one or more slides, perform the following steps:

**1.** Display or select the slide(s) you want to hide. (You can hide slides in Slide, Outline, or Slide Sorter view.)

**2.** Open the Tools menu, and select Hide Slide. If you are in Slide Sorter view, the hidden slide's number appears in a box with a line through it.

**3.** To unhide the slide(s), display or select the hidden slide(s), pull down the Tools menu, and select Hide Slide

In this lesson, you learned how to rearrange the slides in a presentation in either the Slide Sorter or Outline view, and how to hide slides. In the next lesson, you will learn how view a slide show on-screen and fine-tune it.

# Lesson

## 21

# Viewing and Enhancing a Slide Show

*In this lesson, you will learn how to view a slide show on-screen, add timing between slides, and add transitions and builds to animate your slide show.*

An on-screen slide show is a lot like the slide show you can put on by using a slide projector. However, with an on-screen slide show, you can add impressive and professional visual effects (*transitions* and *builds*) that provide smooth and attention-getting movements from one slide to the next.

**Transitions and Builds**   A *transition* is a way of moving from one slide to the next. For example, with a vertical blinds transition, the slide takes on the look of window blinds that turn to reveal the next slide. A *build* displays the bulleted items on a slide, one item at a time, until all the bulleted items are added to the list.

## Viewing an On-Screen Slide Show

You can view a slide show at any time to see how the show will look in real life. To view a slide show, perform the following steps:

**1.** Open the presentation you want to view.

**2.** Or open the View menu, select Slide Show, and click on the Show button. Click on the Slide Show button at the bottom of the presentation window. The first slide in the presentation appears full-screen, as shown in Figure 21.1.

**Figure 21.1** The Slide Show view provides a full-featured slide show.

**3.** To display the next or previous slide, do one of the following:

- To display the next slide, click the left mouse button, or press the right arrow or down arrow key.

- To display the previous slide, click the right mouse button, or click on the left arrow or up arrow key.

- To quit the slide show, press the Esc key.

**The Slide Show Dialog Box**   If you select
Slide Show from the View menu (rather than
clicking on the Slide Show button), you get a
dialog box that offers slide show options. You can
use these options to specify the range of slides you want
to view and to tell PowerPoint how to advance the slides.

# Adding a Slide Transition

In the previous section, you had to click or press an arrow
key to move from one slide to another. If you add timed
transitions to slides, you don't have to click to move from
one slide to the next. The slide show proceeds automatically.

**Transition Effect and Timing**   You can
specify two settings for a transition: the effect and
the timing. The transition effect will apply to the
transition from the previous slide to this slide. The
transition timing will apply to the transition from this slide
to the next slide.

To apply a slide transition to a slide, perform the following steps:

**1.** Open the presentation to which you want to add
transitions.

**2.** Open the View menu, and select Slide Sorter, or
click on the Slide Sorter button at the bottom of the
presentation window.

**3.** Select the slide to which you want to add a transition.

**More Than One**   To select more than one
slide, hold down the Shift key while clicking on
slides. To select all the slides, open the Edit menu,
and choose Select All, or press Ctrl+A.

**4.** Open the Tools menu, and select Transition, or
click on the Transition button in the Slide Sorter
toolbar. The Transition dialog box appears, as
shown in Figure 21.2.

**No Slide Sorter Toolbar?**   If the Slide Sorter
toolbar is not displayed, right-click on any
toolbar, and then click on Slide Sorter.

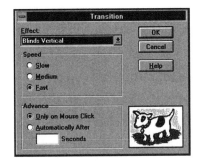

**Figure 21.2**   You can add transition effects and timing to
selected slides.

**5.** Click on the arrow to the right of the **Effect** list, and
click on a transition effect. (Keep an eye on the
preview area to see a demonstration of the effect.)

**6.** In the Speed group, select the desired speed for the
transition to take effect: **S**low, **M**edium, or **F**ast.

**7.** To set a time for automatic slide advance, select one of the options in the Advance group:

**O**nly on Mouse Click moves from this slide to the next slide only when you click the mouse button or press an arrow key.

**A**utomatically After ____ Seconds moves automatically from slide to slide after the specified number of seconds.

**8.** Click on the OK button.

**Quick Effects** To quickly apply a transition effect (without timing), pull down the Transition Effects drop-down list in the Slide Sorter toolbar, and select the desired transition.

## Adding Builds to Slides

A build displays the bulleted points from a slide's Body Area one item at a time on the slide. The build effects are similar to transition effects. To add a build, perform the following steps:

**1.** In Slide Sorter view, select the slide to which you want to add a build.

**2.** Open the Tools menu, and select Build, or click on the Build tool in the Slide Sorter toolbar. The Build dialog box appears, as shown in Figure 21.3.

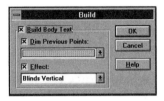

**Figure 21.3** You can have PowerPoint build your slide as your audience looks on.

**3.** Click on the Build Body Text option to turn the Build feature on. An **X** appears in the check box.

**4.** To have bulleted items appear faded as the next bulleted item appears on the slide, select Dim Previous Points, and select the desired dim color from the list.

**5.** To add a special build effect, click on the Effect option, and select the desired effect from the drop-down list. (If you do not select an effect, the items will pop up on the slide.)

**6.** Click on the OK button.

In this lesson, you learned how to run an on-screen slide show presentation, add timed transitions between slides, and add builds to animate your bulleted lists. In the next lesson, you will learn how to create speaker's notes pages.

# Creating Speaker's Notes Pages

*In this lesson, you will learn how to create speaker's notes to help you during the delivery of your presentation.*

The problem with most presentations is that the presenter merely flips from one slide to the next, without telling the audience his point or providing any overview that adds meaning to the slides. To make your slide show a success, you can put together a set of speaker's notes pages that can help you deliver an effective, coherent presentation making sure you do not miss any crucial points you want to highlight.

Each notes page is divided into two parts. A small version of the slide appears at the top of the page, and your notes appear below the slide.

## Creating Speaker's Notes Pages

You already have the slide part of the speaker's notes pages. All you have to do is type the notes. You type notes in Notes Pages view, as follows:

1. Open the presentation for which you want to create speaker's notes pages.

2. Open the View menu, and select Notes Pages, or click on the Notes Pages View button at the bottom of the presentation window. The currently selected slide appears in Notes Pages view, as shown in Figure 22.1.

Slide        Previous slide

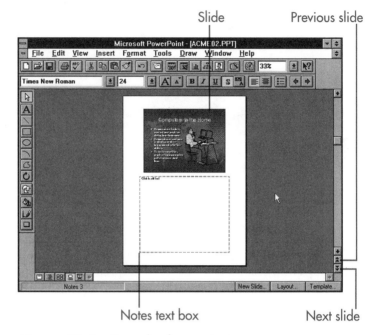

Notes text box        Next slide

**Figure 22.1**   Example of a speaker's notes page.

**3.** Click on the notes text box in the lower half of the notes page to select it.

**4.** To see what you are typing, open the View menu, select Zoom, select a Zoom to percent (100% works well), and click on the OK button.

> **Quick Zoom**   A quicker way to zoom in or out is to open the Zoom Control drop-down list in the Standard toolbar and click on a zoom percent.

**5.** Type the text that you want to use as note material for this slide. (You can include gentle reminders, jokes, supporting data, or explanations as to how this slide fits in the big picture.)

**6.** Click on the Next Slide or Previous Slide button to move to another notes page, and then repeat step 5.

**7.** Format your text as desired. (For details on how to format text, refer to Lessons 10 and 11.)

When you are done, you can print your speaker's notes pages with or without your slides, as explained in Lesson 6.

**Save Your Notes**   When typing your notes, don't forget to save your work on a regular basis. Once you've saved and named your presentation file, saving again is as simple as pressing Ctrl+S.

## Changing the Size of the Slide and Text Box

As explained earlier, each notes page contains two objects: a slide and a text box. You can change the size of either object just as you can change the size of any object in PowerPoint:

**1.** Click on the picture or text box to select it. (If you clicked on the text box, a frame appears around it. Click on the frame to display handles.)

**2.** Move the mouse pointer over one of the object's handles. (Use a corner handle to change both the width and height of the object. Use a side, top, or bottom handle to change only one dimension at a time.)

**3.** Hold down the mouse button, and drag the handle until the object is the desired size and dimensions.

**4.** Release the mouse button.

**Consistent Notes Pages**   To keep the size of the slides and note text boxes consistent on all the notes pages, change the size on the Notes Master. The following section explains how to display and work with the Notes Master.

# Working with the Notes Master

Just as a slide show has a slide master that contains the background and layout for all the slides in the presentation, the Notes Master contains the background and layout for all your notes pages. You can use the Notes Master to do the following:

- Add background information (such as the date, time, or page numbers) and have that information appear on all the notes pages.

- Add a picture, such as a company logo, that will appear on each notes page.

- Move or resize the notes page objects.

- Choose a color scheme or background for the slide (this affects the look of the slide only on the notes pages, not in the presentation itself).

- Set up the Body Area to control the general layout and formatting of the text in the notes area of each notes page.

To change the Notes Master, perform the following steps:

1. Open the View menu, and select Master. The Master submenu appears.

2. Select Notes Master. The Notes Master appears.

3. Change any of the elements of the Notes Master as you would a Slide Master.

In this lesson, you learned how to create a speaker's notes page to help in the delivery of a presentation. In the next lesson, you will learn how to create audience handouts.

# Lesson

# Creating Audience Handouts

*In this lesson, you will learn how to create handouts to pass out to your audience.*

Most presentations move fairly quickly, giving the audience little time to filter through all the data on the slides. Because of this, it is often useful to give the audience handouts or copies of the presentation slides. You can do this by printing an exact replica of your slide show on paper, or by printing several slides per page using audience handouts.

Creating handouts is fairly easy; you simply tell PowerPoint to print audience handouts, placing X number of slides on each page. For example, if you open the File menu and select Print, and then pull down the Print What drop-down list, you see the audience Handouts options shown in Figure 23.1. (For details on how to print, refer to Lesson 6.)

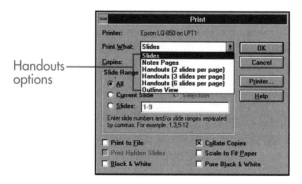

**Figure 23.1** PowerPoint can print 2, 3, or 6 slides per page.

# Displaying the Handout Master

A handout master controls the placement and look of the slides on the audience handouts. The handout master has *slide image placeholders* so you can see where a slide will be placed on a handout. To display the handout master, perform the following steps:

**1.** Open the View menu, and select Master. The Master submenu appears.

**2.** Select Handout Master. The handout master appears, as shown in Figure 23.2.

The handout master shows various slide placement options.

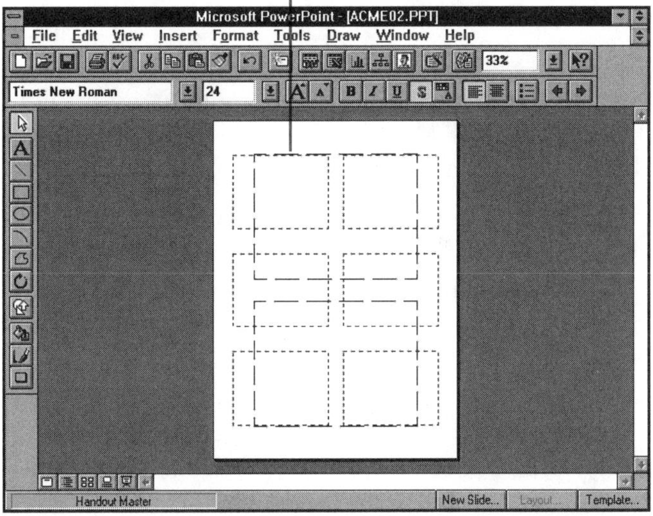

**Figure 23.2** The handout master.

In this lesson, you learned how to create audience handouts to accompany your slide presentation. In the next lesson, you will learn how to use advanced editing tools to check the spelling and ensure consistency in your presentation.

# Lesson

# Using Advanced Editing Tools

*In this lesson, you will learn how to spell check text in your slide presentation, and find and replace text.*

## Checking for Misspellings and Typos

PowerPoint uses a built-in dictionary to spell check your entire presentation, including all slides, outlines, note and handout pages, and all four master views. To check the spelling in your presentation, perform the following steps:

**1.** Open the Tools menu, and select Spelling. The Spelling dialog box appears. (If the spelling dialog box does not appear with a **Start** button displayed, skip step 2.)

> **Menu Bypass** To bypass the **Tools** menu, click on the Spelling button (the button with **ABC** and a check mark on it) in the Standard toolbar, or press F7.

**2.** Click on the Start button to start spell checking. The spell checker starts and then stops on the first word that does not match an entry in the dictionary. (See Figure 24.1.)

Misspelled word

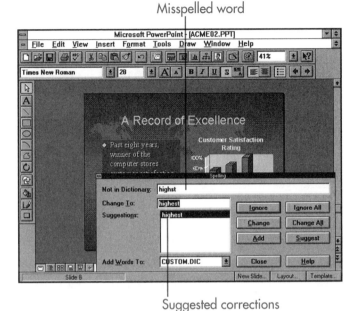

Suggested corrections

**Figure 24.1**   The Spelling dialog box displays the question-able word and suggested corrections.

**3.** If the Spelling dialog box appears displaying a questionable word, select one of these options:

**I**gnore to skip only this occurrence of the word.

**Ig**nore All to ignore every occurrence of the word.

**C**hange to replace only this occurrence of the word with the word in the Change **T**o box. (You can type a correction in the Change **T**o box or select a correct spelling from the Suggestions list.)

Change **A**ll to replace every occurrence of the word with the word in the Change **T**o box. (To insert an entry in the Change **T**o box, type it, or select an entry from the Suggestions list.)

Add to add the word to the dictionary, so the spell checker will not question it again.

Suggest to display a list of suggested words. You can select a word from the list to insert it in the Change To box.

Close to close the Spelling dialog box.

**4.** Repeat step 3 until the spell checker reaches the end of the presentation. A dialog box will appear, telling you that spell checking has been completed.

**5.** Click on the OK button.

# Finding and Replacing Text

If you used a particular word or phrase, but you can't remember which slide you used it on, you can have PowerPoint find the word or phrase for you. You can also have PowerPoint search for a word or phrase and replace one or all instances of the word or phrase.

To search for specific text, perform the following steps:

**1.** Open the Edit menu, and select Find, or press Ctrl+F. The Find dialog box appears.

**2.** In the Find What text box, type the word or phrase you want to search for.

**3.** (Optional) Select either or both of the following options:

Match Case finds text that matches the capitalization in the Find What text box. For example, if you typed Widget, the search will skip **widget**.

Find Whole Words Only skips any occurrences of the text that are a part of another word. For

example, if you typed book, the search will skip
**bookkeeper**.

4. Click on the Find Next button. PowerPoint finds the
   word and highlights it.

**Editing and Formatting Text**    To edit or
format text, simply perform the operation as you
normally would. The Find dialog box remains
on-screen as you work.

5. You can find the next occurrence of the text by
   clicking on the Find Next button again.

6. To close the Find dialog box, click on the Close
   button.

To replace a word or phrase with another word or
phrase, perform the following steps:

1. Open the Edit menu, and select Replace, or press
   Ctrl+H. The Replace dialog box appears, as shown
   in Figure 24.2.

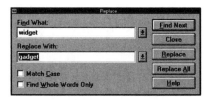

**Figure 24.2**    The Replace dialog box.

2. In the Find What text box, type the word or phrase
   you want to search for.

3. In the Replace With text box, type the word or
   phrase you want to use as the replacement.

**4.** (Optional) Select either or both of the following options:

Match **C**ase finds text that matches the capitalization in the Find What text box.

Find **W**hole Words Only skips any occurrences of the text that are a part of another word.

**5.** Click on one of the following buttons:

**R**eplace replaces one occurrence of the Find What text with the Replace With text.

Replace **A**ll replaces all occurrences of the Find What text (throughout your presentation) with the Replace With text.

**F**ind Next skips the current occurrence of the Find What text and moves to the next occurrence.

**6.** When you are finished replacing text, click on the Close button.

In this lesson, you learned how to check your presentation for misspelled words and typos, and how to find and replace words and phrases. The Appendix that follows contains the basics you need to run Windows and work with PowerPoint.

# Appendix

# Microsoft Windows Primer

*Microsoft Windows is an interface program that makes your computer easier to use by enabling you to select menu items and pictures rather than type commands. Before you can take advantage of it, however, you must learn some Windows basics.*

## Starting Microsoft Windows

To start Windows, do the following:

**1.** At the DOS prompt, type **win**.

**2.** Press Enter.

The Windows title screen appears for a few moments, and then you see a screen like the one in Figure A.1.

**What If It Didn't Work?** You may have to change to the Windows directory before starting Windows; to do so, type **CD \WINDOWS** and press Enter. Then, type **win** and press Enter.

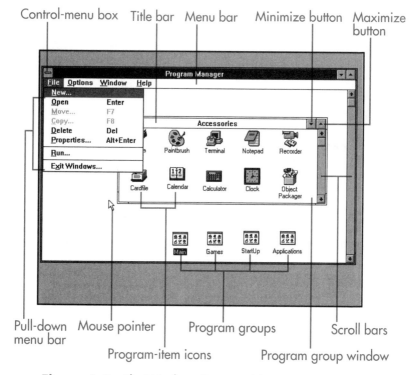

Control-menu box  Title bar  Menu bar  Minimize button  Maximize button

Pull-down menu bar  Mouse pointer  Program groups  Scroll bars

Program-item icons  Program group window

**Figure A.1**  The Windows Program Manager.

## Parts of a Windows Screen

As shown in Figure A.1, the Windows screen contains several unique elements that you won't see in DOS. Here's a brief summary.

- *Title bar*  Shows the name of the window or program.

- *Program group windows*  Contain Program-item icons that allow you to run programs.

- *Icons*  Graphic representations of programs. To run a program, you select its icon.

- *Minimize and Maximize buttons*   Alter a window's size. The Minimize button shrinks the window to the size of an icon. The Maximize button expands the window to fill the screen. When maximized, a window contains a double-arrow *Restore* button, which returns the window to its original size.

- *Control-menu box*   When selected, pulls down a menu that offers size and location controls for the window.

- *Pull-down menu bar*   Contains a list of the pull-down menus available in the program.

- *Mouse pointer*   If you are using a mouse, the mouse pointer (usually an arrow) appears on-screen. It can be controlled by moving the mouse (discussed later in the next section).

- *Scroll bars*   If a window contains more information than it can display, you will see a scroll bar. *Scroll arrows* on each end of the scroll bar allow you to scroll slowly. The *scroll box* allows you to scroll more quickly.

# Using a Mouse

To work most efficiently in Windows, you should use a mouse. You can press mouse buttons and move the mouse in various ways to change the way it acts:

*Point* means to move the mouse pointer onto the specified item by moving the mouse. The tip of the mouse pointer must be touching the item.

*Click on an item* means to move the pointer onto the specified item and press the mouse button once. Unless specified otherwise, use the left mouse button.

*Double-click on an item* means to move the pointer onto the specified item and press and release the left mouse button twice quickly.

*Drag* means to move the mouse pointer onto the specified item and hold down the mouse button while moving the mouse.

Figure A.2 shows how to use the mouse to perform common Windows activities, including running applications and moving and resizing windows.

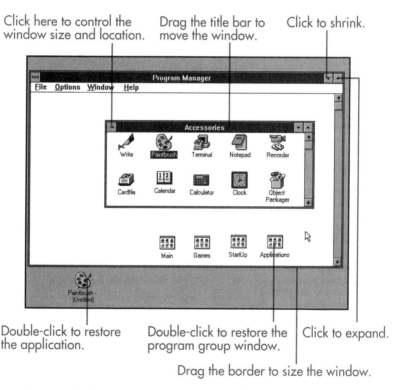

Click here to control the window size and location.

Drag the title bar to move the window.

Click to shrink.

Double-click to restore the application.

Double-click to restore the program group window.

Click to expand.

Drag the border to size the window.

**Figure A.2**  Use your mouse to control Windows.

# Starting a Program

To start a program, simply select its icon. If its icon is contained in a program group window that's not open at the moment, open the window first. Follow these steps:

**1.** If necessary, open the program group window that contains the program you want to run. To open a program group window, double-click on its icon.

**2.** Double-click on the icon for the program you want to run.

# Using Menus

The pull-down menu bar (see Figure A.3) contains various menus from which you can select commands. Each Windows program that you run has a set of pull-down menus; Windows itself has a set, too.

To open a menu, click on its name on the menu bar. Once a menu is open, you can select a command from it by clicking on the desired command.

**Accelerator Keys**   Notice that in Figure A.3, some commands are followed by key names such as **Enter** (for the **O**pen command) or **F8** (for the **C**opy command). These are called *accelerator keys*. You can use these keys to perform the commands without even opening the menu.

Usually, when you select a command, the command is performed immediately. However:

• If the command name is dimmed (gray rather than black), the command is unavailable at the moment, and you cannot choose it.

- If the command name is followed by an arrow, selecting the command will cause another menu to appear, from which you must select another command.

- If the command name is followed by an ellipsis (three dots), selecting it will cause a dialog box to appear. You'll learn about dialog boxes in the next section.

Dimmed options        Accelerator keys

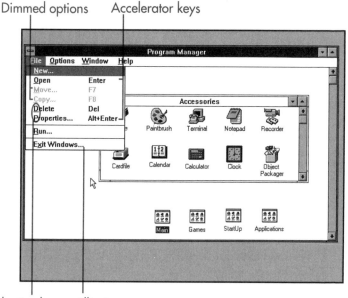

Selection letters  Ellipsis

**Figure A.3**  A pull-down menu lists various commands you can perform.

## Navigating Dialog Boxes

A dialog box is Windows' way of requesting additional information. For example, if you open the File menu and choose Print in PowerPoint, you'll see the dialog box shown in Figure A.4.

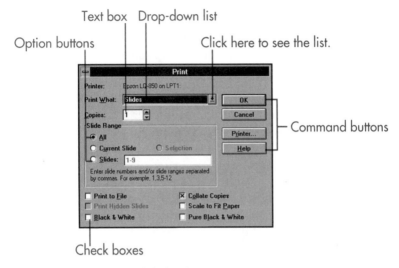

**Figure A.4**  A typical dialog box.

Each dialog box contains one or more of the following elements:

- *List boxes* display available choices. To activate a list, click inside the list box. If the entire list is not visible, use the scroll bar to view the items in the list. To select an item from the list, click on it.

- *Drop-down lists* are similar to list boxes, but only one item in the list is shown. To see the rest of the items, click on the down arrow to the right of the list box. To select an item from the list, click on it.

- *Text boxes* allow you to type an entry. To activate a text box, click inside it. To edit an existing entry, use the arrow keys to move the cursor and the Del or Backspace keys to delete existing characters, and then type your correction.

- *Check boxes* allow you to select one or more items in a group of options. For example, if you are styling text, you can select Bold and Italic to have the text appear in both bold and italic type. Click on a check box to activate it.

- *Option buttons* are like check boxes, but you can select only one option button in a group. Selecting one button unselects any option that is already selected. Click on an option button to activate it.

- *Command buttons* execute (or cancel) the command once you have made your selections in the dialog box. To press a command button, click on it.

## Switching Between Windows

Many times, you will have more than one window open at once. Some open windows may be program group windows, while others may be actual programs that are running. To switch among them, you can:

- Pull down the Window menu, and choose the window you want to view

  OR

- If a portion of the desired window is visible, click on it.

## Controlling a Window

As you saw earlier in this appendix, you can minimize, maximize, and restore windows on your screen. But you can also move them and change their size.

- To move a window, drag its title bar to a different location. (Remember, drag means to hold down the left mouse button while you move the mouse.)

- To resize a window, position the mouse pointer on the border of the window until you see a double-headed arrow; then drag the window border to the desired size.

# Index

## N-O

## P-Q